The Mahdī and Islamic Messianism
Belief in the Coming of the Universal Savior

Āyatollāh Motahharī on Mahdism
Written by Behrūz Mohammadī

His Eminence, the Imām al-Mahdī
The Universal Savior of Humanity
Written by Abdol-Rahīm al-Mūsawī

Mahdism (Islamic Messianism and Belief in
the Coming of the Universal Savior)
Written by Abdol-Karīm Behbahānī

All Selections Translated and Annotated
by Blake Archer Williams

Copyright © 2020 by Blake Archer Williams

All rights reserved. No part of this publication may be reproduced, distributed, or transmitted in any form or by any means, including photocopying, recording, or other electronic or mechanical methods, without the prior written permission of the publisher, except in the case of brief quotations embodied in critical reviews and certain other noncommercial uses permitted by copyright law. For permission requests, write to the publisher, addressed "Attention: - Permissions (Imam Mahdi and Islamic Messianism)," at the email address below.

Lantern Publications
info@lanternpublications.com
www.lanternpublications.com

Ordering Information:
Quantity sales. Special discounts are available on quantity purchases by corporations, associations, and others. For details, contact the distributor at the address below.

Shia Books Australia
www.shiabooks.com.au
info@shiabooks.com.au

ISBN-978-0-6489869-2-8

First Edition

Cover Image: Depicting the active awaiting (*entezār*) of the Mahdi who will take humanity from darkness into the light. Taken at the Imam [or Shah] Mosque, *Naqshe Jahan Square* [Imam Khomeini Square], Esfahan, Iran. © 2020 by Kumayl Virjee, Camfoto Studios.

In the Name of God,
the Most Compassionate, the Most Merciful

Table of Contents

A Note on Transliteration 9

Translator's Foreword 11

Motahharī on the Mahdī and Mahdism 13

His Eminence, the Imām al-Mahdī 91

Islamic Messianism 139

Detailed Table of Contents

Motahharī on the Mahdī and Mahdism 13

Preface 15

1 The Thought of a Universal Savior 17

2 The Idea of Mahdism and the Philosophy of History 27

3 The Era of the Occultation 38

4 Preludes to and Signs of the Advent 50

5 The Uprising 58

6 The Just Order of Post-Adventist Society and its Attributes 72

His Eminence, the Imām al-Mahdī 91

Preface 93

1 The Avowal of the Sunnī Olamā to the Birth of the Mahdī 101

2 The Name and Lineage of Imām Mahdī 107

3 The Characteristics of Imām Mahdī 117

4 The Rank of Imām Mahdī before God 122

5 Imām Mahdī as the Caliph of God ﷻ and the Final Imām 124

6 Jesus will Defer to the Mahdī 126

7 The Banner of Imām Mahdī 129

8 The Generosity and Largesse of Imām Mahdī 130

9 The Miracles of Imām Mahdī 132

Summary and Conclusion 134

Islamic Messianism 139

Preface: 141

1 Proofs of the Belief in Mahdism 146

2 Specific Attributes of the Definition of Mahdism 164

   1. The Covert Birth of the Imām al-Mahdī 165

   2. Investiture to the Imāmate during Childhood 179

   3. The Occultation and Long Life of the Mahdī 190

3 The Value of Belief in the Shīʿa Conception of Mahdism 218

Summary 224

Prayers of God's Peace and Blessings

In keeping with the Islamic practice of showing respect for the name of God, and sending prayers of God's peace and blessings whenever the name of His blessed Prophet, Lady Fātema, and the Twelve Imams is mentioned, as well as for asking God to hasten the reappearance of the Lord of the Age on the Earthly plane, one or more of the following Arabic symbols have been employed throughout the text.

 Used exclusively after the name of God, meaning "the Sublimely Exalted", or, as a prayer, "[May His name be] Sublimely Exalted".

 Used exclusively after the name of the Prophet Mohammad, meaning "May the peace and blessings of God be unto him and unto [the purified and inerrant members of] his family" (i.e. Lady Fātema and the Twelve Imams).

 Used for any of the Twelve Imams or past prophets of God, meaning "May God's peace be unto him".

 Used for two or more of the Twelve Imams or past prophets of God, meaning "May God's peace be unto them".

 Used for Lady Fātema, meaning "May God's peace be unto her".

 Used for a plurality of the Fourteen Immaculates (the Prophet Mohammad, Lady Fātema, and the Twelve Imams), meaning "May God's peace be unto them all collectively".

 Used for the Lord of the Age (the Twelfth Imam), meaning "May God hasten the advent of his noble person".

A Note on Transliteration

The Persian words and Persian words of Arabic origin referred to in this series have been transliterated as they are pronounced (as opposed to all standard academic transliteration systems that transliterate words as they are written). As such, there is no 'system' of transliteration, such as that used by the Library of Congress, by Brill in its Encyclopedia of Islam, or, by the Encyclopedia Iranica, because pronunciations vary from region to region and are at least to some extent subjective. Nevertheless, the reason this approach was preferred is that while it is necessarily somewhat or at least minimally subjective, it has an advantage that more than makes up for this lesser demerit, and that is it that it actually represents the sounds of the words as they are meant to be pronounced. This might not be a factor among a group of orientalist scholars who already know how the words are pronounced and will pronounce the words correctly, despite their transliteration; but the intelligent general reader who is the target audience of this series is not in a position to be able to differentiate between the 'solar' (*shamsi*) and 'lunar' (*qamarī*) letters of the Arabic alphabet, and thus, unlike the orientalist scholar, will pronounce an-Najaf as al-Najaf when he comes across the word spelled as al-Najaf, which would be incorrect. The matter becomes even more complicated when it comes to the name of the august daughter of the Most Noble Prophet, Lady Fātemat oz-Zahrā, the correct pronunciation of whose name is an essential consideration for the Shīʻa faithful. Those who do not know how her name is pronounced will invariably mispronounce it when they see it spelled in accordance with one or another of the standard 'as written' transliteration systems, which spell her name in this way: Fātema al-Zahrā. It is the preclusion of these kinds of pronunciation errors that have motivated us to use the 'as pronounced' approach.

That having been said, there are several Arabic words whose transliteration based on the as-written system(s) has become so prevalent that seeing a transliteration other than what has unfortunately become the standard fare would seem awkward and out of place. In order to preclude this, we have chosen to use what has become standard in such cases. Instances of these cases include the words Quran (which we use over the alternative Qoran or Koran), Muslim (rather than Moslem, which is how the word should be pronounced), and Muhammad (rather than Mohammad, using the letter 'o' to designate the *dhamma* over the *mīm*, this being the correct English equivalent symbol for the phoneme that is symbolized by the *dhamma*).

Translator's Foreword

The impetus to seek God and to submit to His will is an integral part of our primordial disposition or the way in which we have been created (our *fetra*). The Quranic spiritual anthropology tells us that we have two fundamental needs: the need to worship the Creator of the magnificence, beauty, and grandeur of the creation that we are a part of and witness to; and the need to seek guidance concerning how we are to act and live out our lives (individually and in community) in order to conform to that which our Maker has in mind for us. Neither of these needs can be adequately addressed by man's intellect alone, which is the reason for the institution of prophethood and for that special type of knowledge we call revelation, as well as for the institution of the imamate after the ending of the cycle of prophethood. But after the occultation of the Twelfth Imam from the material plane in the year 941 CE (329 AH), the community of the faithful experienced a deep spiritual crisis which it has not been able to fully recover from, with its need for guidance and a fully present *hojja* remaining unfulfilled. This deeply felt unfulfilled need is what gives rise to the desire for the coming of a Divine Guide and to the impetus for the Islamic form of messianism which is called *mahdawīya* (or *mahdavīat* in Persian) or 'Mahdism'.

The Mahdi and Islamic Messianism is comprised of three extended essays that examine this phenomenon in detail. The first essay examines the theological foundations for belief in the Mahdi as explicated by Ayatollah Motahharī. The second essay provides an analysis of the proofs of the true identity and nature of the Mahdi. And the final essay gathers all of the primary hadith sources from Sunni scholarship that discuss the details of the rank, station, attributes and character of the Imām al-Mahdī.

The essay concludes by making a normative evaluation of the difference between the Shī'a conception of Mahdism (whose subject has already been born and is alive, albeit in a state of occultation), and the Sunni conception (which awaits the Mahdi's birth in an indeterminate and distant future).

The outlines of the essays are as follows:

Motahharī on the Mahdī and Mahdism
1 The Thought of a Universal Savior
2 The Idea of Mahdism and the Philosophy of History
3 The Era of the Occultation
4 Preludes to and Signs of the Advent
5 The Uprising
6 The Just Order of Post-Adventist Society and its Attributes

His Eminence, the Imām al-Mahdī
1 The Avowal of the Sunnī Olamā to the Birth of the Mahdī
2 The Name and Lineage of Imām Mahdī
3 The Characteristics of Imām Mahdī
4 The Rank of Imām Mahdī before God
5 Imām Mahdī as the Caliph of God and the Final Imām
6 Jesus will Defer to the Mahdī
7 The Banner of Imām Mahdī
8 The Generosity and Largesse of Imām Mahdī
9 The Miracles of Imām Mahdī

Islamic Messianism
1 Proofs of the Belief in Mahdism
2 Specific Attributes of the Definition of Mahdism
3 The Value of Belief in the Shī'a Conception of Mahdism

Motahharī on the Mahdī and Mahdism
by Behrūz Mohammadī

Preface

On the basis of the teachings of revealed scripture, the idea of Mahdism (or Islamic Messianism) is a universal worldview based on an optimistic outlook concerning the future of humanity which is free of reactionary and ignorant aspirations and of thoughts of personal or national biases. The basic pillars of the idea of Mahdism can be summarized in the following points:

1. Optimism concerning the felicitous livelihood of humanity and its accession to its final state of perfection.
2. Belief in the sovereignty and ultimate rule of reason and its ascendancy over violence and the reign of base and carnal desires.
3. Belief in the ultimate victory of the righteous and God-fearing over tyrants and the corrupt.
4. Belief in the ultimate defeat of mass deceptions and of duplicity and deceit.

In this chapter, we intend to discuss the subject of Mahdism (i.e. Islamic Messianism) and to provide an exposition for all of the truth of the idea of Mahdism with reliance on the writings and thought of Allāma Mortadā Motahharī. And while Allāma Motahharī has not addressed the subject of Mahdism specifically as such (i.e. he has not dedicated an independent treatise to the subject in its own right), we have nonetheless striven to glean his thoughts on the subject from among the vast corpus of his writings in which incidental references to the subject have been made, and to come up with a systematic treatment based on his thoughts on the subject.

1 The Thought of a Universal Savior

Views of the Future
From time immemorial, prophesying the future of humanity and understanding mankind's future and attaining to an understanding of the final outcome of man's worldly existence has been the subject of the attention and investigation of religious and non-religious scholars alike, who have proffered various views concerning the subject. These views can be divided into two broad categories: some believe that prophesying the future is impossible; and contrary to this view, others believe that it is indeed possible to foretell the future fate of mankind, which can be seen from four different perspectives:

1. Evil and corruption are essential and inseparable parts of the human condition; therefore, man's worldly existence is devoid of value and worthy of termination.

2. Humanity will inevitably ultimately fall into the abyss of self-destruction as a consequence of the inexorable march of technological "progress" with respect to the development of the destructive power of weapons of mass destruction; as

such, a dark fate awaits mankind. As Lord Bertrand Russell has stated, 'Some people such as Einstein posit that mankind has already spent its lifecycle and will bring about its destruction at its own hands in the near future.'

3. Evil and corruption are *not* essential and inseparable parts of the human condition but are symptoms of the private ownership of property, which itself is a symptom or manifestation of a level in the evolution of the means of the production of wealth. This deterioration is not subject to human will, but will be supplanted by the inevitable march of the evolution of the means of production and mechanization; as such, the evolution of mechanization and the means of production will set man free and bring him felicity.

4. This view is based on an optimistic outlook with respect to the entirety of the order of nature and on the progressive march toward the perfection of history, confidence in the future, and the rejection of the pessimistic view which posits the end of humanity. This outlook posits the spiritual imperfections and deficiencies of humanity as the root of corruption and degeneration, and holds that while the contemporary era is witness to the reign of aggression and that of base and carnal desires over humanity, that nonetheless, humanity is essentially (or in accordance with his primordial disposition: *bi'l-fitra*) engaged in a process whereby it is taking strides toward his intellectual and moral perfection; and that therefore, a bright and happy future awaits him, in which evil and corruption will be uprooted,

and righteousness, justice, equity and freedom will vanquish violence and aggression, iniquity, tyranny, despotism, and domination.

Belief in a Savior of Humanity – A Universal Belief

The optimistic view of humanity's future and the belief in a savior-reformer, and the belief in the ultimate victory of the forces of justice and good against evil and oppression, and the complete and all-encompassing establishment of the transcendent values of humanity are beliefs which transcend Shī'a Islam and Islam in general. The followers of all [world] religions consider this to be an essential tenet of their faith; just as Christians believe in the Second Coming of the Christ ﷺ, Jews believe in the coming of their Messiah, Hindus are awaiting the advent of Vishnu, Buddhists are awaiting the advent of the Buddha, Zoroastrians believe in the return of the third Saoshyant, the Mongol tribes await the second coming of Chengiz and the Abyssinian Nestorians believe in the coming of their promised King Theodore; and all of the sects within Islam also believe in the coming of a Universal Savior who will establish the reign of justice and make the cause of the righteous prevail throughout the earth.

The Bases for the Idea of Mahdism

The idea of Mahdism (or the ideation of the coming of a Universal Savior within Islamicate civilization) which is one of the glad tidings given by the teachings of Islam to its adherents has its roots in the Quran and the *sunna* (the normative practice of the Prophet ﷺ of Islam).

1. The Quran

As the sole divine source within Islam, the Quran looks upon the [totality of] the history and ultimate end of humanity with optimism and posits mankind as being endowed with a kind of innate propensity which predisposes him to values such as sincerity, trustworthiness, equity and fairness, all of which will ultimately prevail over corruption and [moral] degradation, and [posits] the future of the world as culminating with the coming of a universal savior who will act in the interests of the righteous within the rank and file of humanity. And while it is true that this conception is not explicitly and directly expressed in some of the verses (*āya*, plural, *āyāt*: divine signs, individual units of revelation) of the Quran, interpretations which have reached us from the [Fourteen] Immaculates ﷻ (*ma'sūmīn*)[1] by way of historical reports, make it clear that such verses imply the coming of a universal savior and his reign of peace over the whole world.

هُوَ الَّذِي أَرْسَلَ رَسُولَهُ بِالْهُدَىٰ وَدِينِ الْحَقِّ لِيُظْهِرَهُ عَلَى الدِّينِ كُلِّهِ وَلَوْ كَرِهَ الْمُشْرِكُونَ

---

[1] The Prophet Mohammad ﷺ, his daughter Lady Fātema ﷻ, and the Twelve Imams ﷻ, all of whom are held by the Shī'a to be immaculate, i.e. inerrant as well as sinless.

1. [9:33] He it is who has sent forth His Apostle with the [task of spreading] guidance and the religion of truth, to the end that He may cause it to prevail over all [false] religion - however hateful this may be to those who ascribe divinity to aught beside God ﷻ.

وَلَقَدْ كَتَبْنَا فِي الزَّبُورِ مِن بَعْدِ الذِّكْرِ أَنَّ الْأَرْضَ يَرِثُهَا عِبَادِيَ الصَّالِحُونَ

2. [21:105] And indeed, after having exhorted [man], We laid it down in all the books of divine wisdom that My righteous servants shall inherit the earth.

وَنُرِيدُ أَن نَّمُنَّ عَلَى الَّذِينَ اسْتُضْعِفُوا فِي الْأَرْضِ وَنَجْعَلَهُمْ أَئِمَّةً وَنَجْعَلَهُمُ الْوَارِثِينَ

3. [28:5] But it was Our will to bestow Our favor upon those [very people] who were deemed [so] utterly low in the land, and to make them forerunners in faith, and to make them heirs [to Pharaoh's glory, i.e. that they will inherit the earth].

قَالَ مُوسَىٰ لِقَوْمِهِ اسْتَعِينُوا بِاللَّهِ وَاصْبِرُوا ۖ إِنَّ الْأَرْضَ لِلَّهِ يُورِثُهَا مَن يَشَاءُ مِنْ عِبَادِهِ ۖ وَالْعَاقِبَةُ لِلْمُتَّقِينَ

4. [7:128] [And] Moses said unto his people: "Turn unto God ﷻ for aid, and have patience in adversity. Verily, all

the earth belongs to God: He gives it as a heritage - to such as He wills of His servants; and the future belongs to the God-fearing!"

وَعَدَ اللَّهُ الَّذِينَ آمَنُوا مِنكُمْ وَعَمِلُوا الصَّالِحَاتِ لَيَسْتَخْلِفَنَّهُمْ فِي الْأَرْضِ كَمَا اسْتَخْلَفَ الَّذِينَ مِن قَبْلِهِمْ وَلَيُمَكِّنَنَّ لَهُمْ دِينَهُمُ الَّذِي ارْتَضَىٰ لَهُمْ وَلَيُبَدِّلَنَّهُم مِّن بَعْدِ خَوْفِهِمْ أَمْنًا ۚ يَعْبُدُونَنِي لَا يُشْرِكُونَ بِي شَيْئًا ۚ وَمَن كَفَرَ بَعْدَ ذَٰلِكَ فَأُولَٰئِكَ هُمُ الْفَاسِقُونَ

5. [24:55] God 🕌 has promised those of you who have attained to faith and do righteous deeds that, of a certainty, He will cause them to accede to power on earth, even as He caused [some of] those who lived before them to accede to it; and that, of a certainty, He will firmly establish for them the religion which He has been pleased to bestow on them; and that, of a certainty, He will cause their erstwhile state of fear to be replaced by a sense of security [seeing that] they worship Me [alone], not ascribing divine powers to aught beside Me. But all who, after [having understood] this, choose to deny the truth - it is they, they who are truly iniquitous!

2. The Sunnaᵗ (the Paradigmatic example of the Prophet ﷺ)[2]

The *hadīth* reports[3] concerning Mahdism are so numerous that they have been compiled in books that run into several volumes. Thus, a comprehensive treatment of these reports is beyond the scope of this chapter. Here it will suffice our purposes to cite only a few of the reports which have reached us from the Most Noble Prophet ﷺ, and upon whose soundness and reliability there is consensus between the Sunni and the Shī'a.

1. "If there were only one day remaining of the life of the world, God would lengthen the duration of that day to such an extent until a man from my progeny rises in insurrection [against the forces of oppression]." This *hadīth* report portrays the ideal of the prophets as an actual fact whose occurrence is a necessity.

2. "The Imam al-Mahdī will arise out of my community while the danger of humanity endangers the earth."

3. "The Imam Mahdī will fill the world with justice and equity just as it will have become filled with injustice and oppression."

Consequences of Belief in a Universal Savior

---

[2] This is discussed more comprehensively in subsequent chapters.

[3] *Hadīth*: a report setting forth a saying or deed of the Prophet ﷺ, or in Shi'i usage, of one of the Twelve Imams, or Lady Fātema as well.

1. Optimism and Hope in the Future

Hope in the future together with expending effort and striving [to achieve one's future goals] are intrinsic attributes of all mankind that are the equivalent to life itself, (such that their absence is an indicator of a spiritual or emotional malady); hope plays a vital role in man's life, ensuring that man maintains his relationship to the future and plans his actions accordingly. As the Prophet ﷺ has stated, "If there were no [such thing as] hope, no mother would suckle her young, and no one would plant any trees."

But [working] against hope there is despondency and hopelessness which drive one to despair, debilitation and annihilation, and which saps one's spiritual life-force.

Today, modern man is afflicted with spiritual crises, economic stagnation, and the like, all of which sap the spirit of hope from him and allow despondency and despair to dominate him. Whereas based on the teachings which fall under the general rubric of Mahdism, hope in the future is accepted as a universal and unquestionable principle; and more than anything, this idea is comprised of optimism relative to the entire natural order, the evolutionary nature of history and assurance in [the ultimately positive outcome of] the future, and the rejection of any pessimism concerning man's final fate.

In all truth, a person who has been cultivated under the auspices of the divine teachings [of Islam] and who has faith [in the world of the unseen] and believes himself to be the beneficiary of aid from the beyond (the world beyond the ken of ordinary human perception), believes that while the realm of this world is one of toil and various hardships, that nonetheless, the abode of humanity will not be destroyed by the whirlwind of world events, and that ultimately, perfect happiness and prosperity will be man's trophy in the future, and that with the coming of the Universal Savior, mankind will bask on the shores of security, prosperity and comfort.

Thus, such a person is like someone who is crossing a tunnel, irrespective of whether or not he will reach the other side. With this outlook, while the tunnel is innately dark, artificial lighting has been affixed throughout its length, and there is a vast and bright open expanse at the end of the tunnel whose light is assuredly natural. Hope in the ultimate prevailing of good and the establishment of universal justice illuminates the artificial lighting of the tunnel in the era of the occultation,[4] so that the path to reaching the awaited goals of justice and peace and freedom (in their true and real sense) is lit, so that a bright future is placed before humanity as a result.

2. The Role played by belief in Mahdism in the Social Context

The glad tidings given by the Noble Quran and by the Most Noble Prophet ﷺ concerning the coming of a universal savior by the name of the Mahdī ﷵ had a great impact on the social movements and upheavals and insurrections throughout Islamic

---

[4] The era where humanity is no longer in direct contact with the Mahdī, who went into occultation in the 329th year of the Islamic lunar calendar (941 of the Christian era).

history from its very beginning, some of which had positive effects, and others, such as movements around false claims to being the Mahdī, having negative consequences. For example, Mokhtār ath-Thaqafī understood that if he were to continue his insurrectionary movement on his own for revenge of the blood of Imam Hosayn ﷺ, the people would not follow him. Thus, by adopting the slogan that "Mohammad b. al-Hanafīya is the promised Mahdī" and that Mokhtār was his representative, he gave his movement more popular appeal, and caused many who believed in his slogan to flock to his side. Similarly, when an-Nafs az-Zakīya rose up in insurrection, many pledged allegiance to him because they [falsely] believed him to be the Mahdī. In this way, his movement became more popular and grew stronger.

Another area in which belief in the idea of Mahdism has been influential is in the formation of sects. For example, on the occasion of the death of the Immaculate Imams ﷺ, some of their followers thought them to be the promised Mahdī and refused to accept the fact that they had died and left the worldly plane, believing instead that they had merely become occulted from physical sight. Thus, these beliefs gave rise to various sects such as the Wāqefīya, the Nāwūsīya, and so on after the attaining to martyrdom of those great Imams. In recent times too, from time to time, we see people laying claim to being the Mahdī in different corners of the world, such as Ahmad Qādīyānīya and Ahmad "the Bāb" (portal), [who claimed to be the *bāb* or portal to the Imam, then claimed to be the returned Imam al-Mahdī himself;] some people would gather around these false claimants, thus giving rise to sects such as the Bahāīs.

We should of course bear in mind that in the formation of such millenarian sects, the idea of Mahdism is invariably used as a pretext to mask the real motivations for the formation of such sects which usually have to do with material benefit and other political considerations; and this is especially so in the case of the advent of sects such as the Wāqefīya and the Bābīya (which morphed into Bahāism) whose impetus of origination was not, strictly speaking, belief in Mahdism.

2 The Idea of Mahdism and the Philosophy of History

The philosophy of history consists of knowledge of the vicissitudes and changes of a given society because [knowledge of] the nature of history reveals the principles which govern [the social life of] humanity and the primary forces which turn the pages of history.

The philosophy of history is one of the important principles of Quranic thinking and [as such] of a *towhīdic*[5] worldview, which

---

[5] *Towhīd* (the unicity or exclusivity of worship); *towhīdic*: The Islamic conception of monotheism: 1. The unicity of the creatorship of the universe; 2. The unicity of the order of creation; 3. The exclusivity of providential lordship (*towhīd-e rūbūbīat*). God's integral (*towhīd*) order of creation. Fidelity (*towhīd*) and Infidelity (*sherk*) to the Exclusivity of God's Providential Lordship in the Social Order. *Towhīd* is the first principle of the Islamic faith and is usually translated as Monotheism or as the unicity of God ﷻ. *Towhīd* refers to the unicity of God ﷻ not just in His capacity as Creator (i.e. unicity of Creatorship), but also refers to the seamlessness of the order within creation (including man's social

consists of three components: the purpose and bearing of the movement of history; the mechanism(s) which put history into motion; and the path and direction of history.

A detailed analysis of these three postulates is beyond the scope of this chapter, but what is relevant to the idea of Mahdism is the investigation of the following questions: are the changes that occur in history a series of facts which take place by accident or are they a series of naturally occurring phenomena? Do the changes that occur in history take place in accordance with general principles and scientifically [discoverable] laws, or is this not the case? There are two positions concerning the answers to these questions.

1. Society is only a collection of individuals, each with their own specific and unique nature, and the collectivity of the phenomena

---

order) as a corollary of that act of creation. Thus, *towhīd* refers to the integrality of creation with the social order that is intended for that creation by God: the integral (*towhīdic*) Islamic society. The *towhīdic* worldview is the Islamic vision of monotheism; it is an integral vision of the universe where belief in the unicity of creatorship is seamlessly intertwined and combined with the belief that providential lordship over the world and the individual and collective affairs of man are the exclusive domain of God ﷻ. It is belief in the unicity of creatorship and the integrality of the order of creation with the will of the One Creator, which is the necessary corollary of this unicity. *Towhīd* is the primary creedal tenet of Islam which holds that God ﷻ is the sole creator of the world, and that He has exclusivity of providential lordship over His creation, i.e. the exclusive right to sovereignty and control over it.

which come about as a result of these individual proclivities result in a series of accidental events, and these events give rise to the changes and developments of history.

2. Society has its own nature and character which is independent of the individuals which comprise its component parts, and behaves in accordance with its own nature and character. The character of society is not identical with [the sum of] the character of the individuals [of whom it is comprised]; rather, a real and actual personality emerges for society from the social and cultural actions [of groups and individuals]. Accordingly, society too is governed by laws and criteria, and its actions and reactions are explainable by a series of universal laws and general principles, so that history does indeed have a governing philosophy and laws by which it acts, and can thus be the subject of intellectual deliberation and a source from which lessons can be learned. This is also the position of the Noble Quran, where it characterizes the developments of history as divine traditions (*sonan-e elāhī*) which fall within [the aegis of] universal laws and principles, and the life-stories of tribes and nations of the past are presented as learning lessons for other peoples [to whom the Quran addresses itself]:

تِلْكَ أُمَّةٌ قَدْ خَلَتْ ۖ لَهَا مَا كَسَبَتْ وَلَكُم مَّا كَسَبْتُمْ ۖ وَلَا تُسْأَلُونَ عَمَّا كَانُوا يَعْمَلُونَ

[2:134] Now those people have passed away; unto them shall be accounted what they have earned, and unto you, what you have earned; and you will not be judged on the strength of what they did.

Thus, the Noble Quran vehemently rejects the notion of the purposelessness and accidental nature of history, and stipulates that an eternal law governs the fate of nations.

$$\text{فَهَلْ يَنظُرُونَ إِلَّا سُنَّتَ الْأَوَّلِينَ ۚ فَلَن تَجِدَ لِسُنَّتِ اللَّهِ تَبْدِيلًا ۖ وَلَن تَجِدَ لِسُنَّتِ اللَّهِ تَحْوِيلًا}$$

> [35:43] Do they expect anything other than [God's] way with those who lived before. No change wilt thou ever find in God's way; yea, no deviation wilt thou ever find in God's way!

Nonetheless, the Quran reminds us concerning the traditions of history that mankind can change his destiny for the better or for the worse based on [his conformance with] divine traditions; and that while history is governed by categorical sacred laws, this fact in no way negates man's role and his freedom of will and action within it.

$$\text{إِنَّ اللَّهَ لَا يُغَيِّرُ مَا بِقَوْمٍ حَتَّىٰ يُغَيِّرُوا مَا بِأَنفُسِهِمْ}$$

> [13:11] Verily, God ﷻ does not change men's condition unless they change their own condition.

The Explanation and Justification of the theory of the Developmental Evolution of History

If an ideology posits society as having a nature and character of its own, and posits it as a creature which is alive and which evolves and goes through progressive stages of development, then it is incumbent on such an ideology to explain and justify the progressive development of history. Now there are two views which are discernible in this regard which result from two different anthropologies and two views of the identity and innate aptitudes of man.

1. The "Means [of Production]" Perspective and Dialectical Thinking

In the dialectical thought [of historical materialism], mankind is bereft of any human characteristic in his essence, and there is nothing in his makeup which distinguishes him qualitatively from other animals, nor is there anything which is original to him and uniquely his, be this in his understanding and vision, or in his emotions or propensities. In this conception, man is likened to nothing but an empty vessel which is filled from without by external social forces, and whose personality is based on social and particularly on economic factors. Accordingly, what is real in man is his animalistic attributes, according to this anthropology, which posits man as a creature who is driven by material considerations and who is subject to the ineluctable forces of nature, and of those of the means of production in particular, which imprison him in the economic conditions of his era, where his sense of right and wrong, his desires, judgments and thoughts are all simply products and reflections of his natural and economic environment, to which influences he is bound and outside of which influences he has no will and therefore cannot tread. In his origins, so the theory goes, man was a raw material, and it is the [forces of] production of society and the means by which that production is attained which gives shape to this raw material; a shape that is appropriate to the type of work that is taking place in society, and appropriate to the kind of means and instruments [and labor] which the production of this work necessitates.

According to the dialectical thought [of historical materialism]:

1. Nature is in a state of constant flux and is never in a steady state.

2. All parts of nature are seamlessly interconnected and each part influences and is influenced by all other parts, such that our understanding of nature is correct only when we envision everything as interconnected and do not analyze and study things as separate and individual entities.

3. The impetus for [societal] change comes from the tensions [that exist within society], such that everything naturally tends towards its negation and antithesis and cultivates it within itself. With the growth of negating factors, two elements are arrayed [in opposition] within a given entity: the original and stabilizing forces which want to maintain things as they are, and the forces of negation which want to transform the entity into its antithesis.

4. The inner tension within phenomena tends to increase and gains steam until it reaches its peak, i.e. it reaches the limit of tension and conflict possible, to the point where quantitative changes [in tension] take a revolutionary leap and bring about a qualitative change; and the conflict is resolved in favor of the new forces and against the old, and the thesis is turned into its antithesis, after which the same process repeats itself, where the antithesis which has vanquished the thesis [after a process of 'the negation of the negation on the part of conservative forces) becomes the synthesis, which immediately becomes a new thesis, which in turn fosters and engenders its own antithesis, and so on.

And so this view posits the process and nature of change in nature as moving in this fashion, moving from one developmental stage to another. But because nature is without purpose and is not searching for its perfection, it tends to seeks its destruction, and this [stage of] destruction in turn seeks *its* destruction, and [the stage of] the destruction of the destruction, which is a synthesis of the two previous stages obtains, and this state of affairs goes on *ad infinitum* in what is characterized as the "development" of history which occurs in an ineluctable or predestinarian fashion.

According to this view, history is a part and parcel of nature, and while its constructive elements are human beings, its behavior is governed by the same laws of nature, and like nature, is subject to the eternal tension between thesis and antithesis, where every phenomenon is turned into its antithesis, and then to the antithesis of the antithesis in a developmental chain. Thus, history is posited as an eternal flux, and as an eternal conflict between man and nature, and as an eternal conflict between man and society, and as an eternal conflict between progressive and reactionary forces and groupings which ultimately ends in a revolutionary upheaval and the victory of the progressive forces over the forces of reaction.

Thus, tension and conflict builds between the dark forces of reaction and the enlightened forces of development and progress and reaches its peak, which is the point at which a revolutionary explosion takes place, and society takes a giant leap forward, with the forces of revolution replacing the *ancien régime* with the forces of the new order, ushering in a new historical era. This new era will in its turn have the same fate as the one it replaced by new people who were in search of and have become endowed with the latest means of production. And again, this generation will also lose the ability to solve social problems due to the [technological march forward and its consequent] increase in the level of production, plunging society into another dead-end and another crisis and conflict, bringing about the necessity for a revolutionary change in the economic and social order. This process continues in the same fashion, so that history, like nature, is in a constant state of flux between the two poles of thesis and antithesis, each new stage being a synthesis of the previous two stages, the antithesis of whose original stage was latent within the stage that ultimately replaced it. And as stated before, this state of affairs goes on *ad infinitum* in what is characterized as the "development" of history which occurs in an ineluctable or predestinarian fashion.

One of the important attributes of this way of thinking (which has become a pretext of sorts for the feeble-minded among the Muslim community) is that these unfortunate souls consider any and all social currents which lay the groundwork for revolution or add to the speed of the developmental process as hallowed and sacred. This is inclusive of anything that brings about chaos, as this engenders dissatisfaction [among the masses] and widens the social fissures and adds fuel to the social fire; and this is because [in their feeble minds,] the end justifies the means. This sort of destructive thinking is fostered as opposed to incremental changes and reforms, which are considered to be undesirable as such measures dampen the pace of the revolutionary struggle and ultimately delay the revolution to come.

2. The *Fetric*[6] and Humane Perspective

According to this view, while man does not have a human character from its very genesis, but at the same time, the seed of a series of insights and proclivities are contained within him, and he is like a sapling which contains specific abilities in terms of what it will grow into, so that it does not have a need for external stimuli, as does the "raw material" of the historical materialists, for taking form. Rather, its needs are like that of a sapling for soil and water and light and heat, by means of which it reaches to fruition that purpose which is contained within itself.

---

[6] *Fetric:* Having to do with one's primordial disposition and orientation; having to do with the way in which man has been created; intrinsic, innate.

Therefore, mankind is a creature who is in possession of a divine inward disposition and who is equipped with a primordial nature which recognizes and seeks justice, and who is self-governing and free of any natural predetermination. According to this anthropology, only human values are authentically human and are present in man as a series of intrinsic propensities within his nature, as a result of which he seeks transcendent ideals such as truth and justice and the higher values and ideals of the humanities. By virtue of the power of his intellect, man can design his own society and not surrender to blind fate; and by virtue of his free will and power of choice, he can realize his mental plans. And in this arena, that special knowledge which we call revelation rushes to his aid as a guide to and guardian of these inwardly-held human values.

In this view of man, philosophically speaking, society's relation to individuals and objects is truly compound; and in terms of characteristics and attributes, society is an agglomeration of the high and low values of individuals plus a series of other attributes which continue to exist in the ongoing life of society which is "humanity at large" and which is not affected by the death of individual human beings.

According to this view, then, history, like nature herself, is in a state of change and development consequent to its own essentiality, and is moving in the direction that is demanded by the perfection of its essence. But with this difference, that the nature of history is not a purely material nature, but like the nature of individual human beings, is a binary pairing of matter and spirit, and the progressive development of history encompasses all of the spiritual and cultural aspects of human existence and is moving in the direction of the emancipation of man from his environmental and social constraints. Because man's path to his perfection is comprehensive and all-encompassing, his development will gradually reduce his environmental and social dependencies, and will attain to a kind of deliverance which equates to a dependence on faith and correct belief; and in the future, man will reach complete freedom, meaning he will be completely dependent on [the tenets and practice of his] faith and on the correct belief and ideological path.

From this vantage, the inner conflict between man's lower desires and urges and the dictates of his reason is among his attributes, as is the more general struggle between his earthly aspects and his transcendent and heavenly ones, meaning the conflict between lower desires and instincts which have no purpose other than a limited individual one which is ephemeral, and drives which move man upward and who want to free man from the confines of his [excessive, radical and blameworthy] individualism, and to encompass the entirety of humanity as [the beneficiary of] its objectives, and to posit the noble aims of ethical conduct, and of religious, scientific and rational ideals as its ultimate goals. In fact, the battle has always been between persons who set transcendent values for themselves and are not bound to selfish desires but to [the tenets of] faith and correct belief on one side, and selfish human beings who are not bound to any behavioral norms and who are no better than animals in their looking out only for their own self-interests, and whose life is devoid of any noetic existence or of any of the high ideals that make us human; and this struggle has gradually taken on an ideological character, and man draws ever closer to the stages of his perfection in terms of his human values and ideals, i.e. drawing closer to the ideal man and to the ideal society, to the point where ultimately governance and justice will merge and fuse, i.e. a stage will be reached where the perfection of human ideals will reign, and this stage is referred to in Islamic terminology as the Reign of the Mahdī, where the reign of the selfish and animalistic forces of idolatry and falsehood will be vanquished and uprooted.

3 The Era of the Occultation

From the point of view of the Imāmīya (Twelver) Shī'a, and with reliance on *motewāter*[7] prophetic *hadīth* reports and the testimony of history and multiple narrators of *hadīth*, the promised Mahdī was born on the night of Friday the 15th of Sha'bān in the 255th lunar year of the Islamic calendar.

In so far as this birthday is, on the basis of the prophecies of the Prophet and of the Immaculate Imams, the birthday of

---

[7] *Motewāter* - The highest possible classification of reliability of a hadīth report. A *hadīth* report is considered *motewāter* (having reached the threshold of *tawātor*) when it has been transmitted with a frequency of transmission through different chains of narrators in exactly the same way to the extent that there can remain no doubt concerning the authenticity and reliability of the text in question.

the destroyer of tyrants and of the social orders established by illegitimate powers (*tāghūt*),⁸ the occasion instilled fear in the hearts of the powers of oppression, such that just as Pharaoh feared the birth of Moses ﷺ and was intent on finding and destroying him, the agents and spies of the Abbāsid caliph al-Mo'tasem would monitor the house of Imam Hasan al-Askarī ﷺ (the Mahdī's father), and enter it in all times of day and night in order to search it for the possible presence of a newborn child. Consequently, his Eminence the Hojjat⁹ ﷺ was born and lived in secrecy away from the reach of the Abbāsid agents who were intent on killing him. And so, he was never able to appear in public and was not seen by the general population but only by a few select companions of Imam Hasan al-Askarī ﷺ, and this state of affairs continued until the martyrdom of Imam Hasan al-Askarī ﷺ, shortly after which the period of the *ghaybaʻ* or the occultation of the Imam al-Mahdī from the physical plane began.

The occultation of the Imam al-Mahdī ﷺ and his absence from the physical plane is divided into two stages: a short period of about 70 years (260 Lunar/ 872 CE to 329 Lunar/ 939 CE) which is known as the Lesser Occultation (*al-ghaybaʻ as-soghrā*), and the longer period which started with the ending of the Lesser Occultation and continues to this day.

---

⁸ *Tāghūt:* the false or illegitimate authority of anyone or anything other than God; idolatry and heathenism; social orders based on idol worship of any kind.

⁹ A title of the Mahdī meaning 'the Proof [of God ﷻ on Earth]'.

In the period of the Lesser Occultation which lasted almost 70 years, the Imam al-Mahdī ﷻ was in contact with his followers (*Shī'a*), and responded to the problems of the community by the intermediacy of Four Deputies (*nāyeb*, plural *nawwāb*). These four deputies were:

1. Othmān b. Sa'īd al-'Amrī (260/ 874 – 875)
2. Mohammad b. Othmān al-'Amrī (d. 304/ 916 – 917)
3. Al-Hosayn b. Rūh an-Nowbakhtī (d. 326/ 937 – 938)
4. Ali b. Mohammad as-Samarrī (d. 329/ 940 – 941)

During this time these specifically designated individuals acted on behalf of the Imam in all matters having to do with the community of their faithful followers, thus preparing them for the Greater Occultation.

After the period of the Lesser Occultation, the period of the Greater Occultation began (329 Lunar/ 939 CE), in which the connection of the Imam with the people, limited as it was, was severed, and the people were duty-bound (*mowazzaf*) at that point to refer their questions and problems to the general deputies of the Imam al-Mahdī, who are the fully-qualified magisters or *foqahā*, the doctors of theology and sacred jurisprudence. This period (which continues to the present) was and continues to be the greatest arena for the assaying of mankind, acting as an acid test and sieve for the separation of the faithful. In this period, mankind has religious duties to God ﷻ over and above those prescribed as obligatory, the most important of which is awaiting the Mahdī's advent or return. When the divine *mashī'a* (Corbin translates the word as 'innate divine Will') is realized with the advent of the Imam al-Mahdī ﷻ, the veil will be rended away from the Imam, revealing his presence.

A detailed analysis of the important considerations concerning the era of the occultation is outside of the scope of this introductory book; we will therefore briefly attend to the main points.

The Order of the Imāmate[10] and the Occultation

In the Shī'a understanding of the term, the imāmate is an office similar to that of the highest degree of prophethood, whose office holder is vested [by God] with all of the responsibilities of prophethood with the exception of the function of the bringing of revelation and sacred law, and is considered to be the undisputed religious, [political, and spiritual] leader of the community. [This office must necessarily be endowed with such functions and have a leadership endowed with such qualities because the Shī'a believe that] after the passing of the Prophet ﷺ from the earthly plane, God, the All-Knowing, did not abandon humanity to its own devices and has necessarily selected and designated leaders for the outward and inward guidance of mankind until the last moment of the life of this world [i.e. until the Day of Resurrection]. Therefore, the Earth will never be

---

[10] The imamate is the name given to the Shī'a conception of the religio-political leadership of the community of the faithful.

without a *hojjat*[11] (proof [of God ﷻ on Earth]), as his Eminence Imam Ali ؏ has stated:

> Verily, the Earth will not be without a *hojjat* of God's, be he manifest and known or hidden from sight and unknown, so that God's *hojjat* is not invalidated and His signs are not obliterated. And how many of these are there, and where do they abide? I swear [upon my oath] to God! They are few in number and have a high [spiritual] rank with God ﷻ. God ﷻ maintains His [evidentiary and testamentary] proofs [for and against mankind on the Day of Judgment] and signs by means of them [i.e. by means of their exemplary presence among mankind], [and does so in series, such that] they each entrust [the functions of this office] to others [who are] like themselves [in terms of their *hojjatic* functions], who will plant [this trust] in their own hearts.[12]

---

[11] al-Hojjat: the Proof (of God ﷻ on Earth) [36:12] ... *For of all things do We take account in a manifest Imām* (imāmin mobīn) [who shall be called to testify and provide evidence on all matters on the Day of Judgment]. This is the meaning of the word *hojjatollāh* or God's proof, which is one of the names given to the Imāms by the Quran: The *hojjat* is the perfect embodiment and clear evidence of all truth on Earth and the conclusive argument and evidentiary proof against all falsehood on Judgement Day.

[12] *Nahj ol-Balāgha*, Wisdom # 147.

Thus, Shaykh Ashraf states that the best leader is one who is a perfect exemplary model in terms of his wisdom and knowledge [of the religious sciences] and his diligence and practice with respect to God's [ordinances], and such a person is necessary in every era, even if he is to be in a state of concealment.

According to the teachings of Shī'a Islam, the promised savior is also one who is vested with the office of the imāmate, and whose presence is necessary [for mankind in order to provide humanity with perfect guidance and in order to perfect God's plan by way of His grace to mankind.] Additionally, the Imam al-Mahdī is also burdened with the responsibilities of the Most Noble Prophet with respect to the inner guidance of humanity, guiding it in its development and growth and leading humanity home to its intended spiritual perfection, thereby bringing the ideals of prophethood to fruition.

Constructive Responsibilities during the Era of Occultation

There is no doubt that mankind is burdened with greater responsibilities in the era of occultation where mankind is deprived of the benefits of the physical presence of the Immaculate Imam. Some of these responsibilities include: the laying of the groundwork for the advent of the savior, working on the purification of one's own soul and that of others, and most importantly, awaiting the advent.

Awaiting the Advent

The principle of being in wait of the advent is derived from the Quranic principle of the prohibition against despairing of the spirit of God, which means that the believer must never and under no condition lose hope in God's grace, and must never surrender to the temptation of despondency and hopelessness.

But idiomatically, the expression 'being in wait of the advent' refers to the state of someone who is not content with the current [political and moral] order and who strives for the establishment of a better one. The person who is in wait of the advent believes that a day will come when the hardships of the righteous and those who persevere with patience and forbearance will come to an end, and that one must not be subdued and defeated by the forces of corruption and oppression. Thus, there are two elements to being in wait: hope and desire. Hope in the sense that the victory of the enemies of God's religion and of humanity is considered to be temporary and is not something to be surrendered to; and desire in the sense that while the advent does indeed have a supernatural aspect, it is nevertheless brought about [in part] as a result of the efforts of a group of worthy and like-minded individuals [who lay the foundations for the Mahdī's return and come to his aid upon his advent].

According to the teachings of the idea of Mahdism, awaiting the advent of the savior is a virtue that has a privileged position and is considered to be a kind of religious duty and practice, as has been stated by the Most Noble Prophet:

One of the most exalted practices of my community is awaiting God's [will to allow for] the advent [of the Mahdī].

Therefore, it is incumbent on everyone to consider the waiting for the advent to be a religious duty and to put it into practice with a religious dedication of purpose, and to benefit from the results of this practice.

1. Destructive Awaiting

Some believe that the advent will be like an explosion and will occur only after the proliferation and intensification of iniquity and oppression and the ruination [of God's order], and that the savior's advent and reforms will only take place when the righteous will have been completely vanquished by the forces of false and illegitimate authority. According to this way of thinking, corruption and oppression and all manner of abominations will intensify to a critical mass, bringing the probability of the advent ever closer, and this state of affairs will reach a pinnacle of explosion, which paves the way for the appearance of the Mahdī. [And this way of thinking is brought about and justified by the underlying false assumption that] 'legitimate ends justify illegitimate means'. And so – the thinking goes – the best way to hasten the advent and the best posture to take while awaiting it, is the promotion and promulgation of corruption.

Those who hold such views look to the righteous and those who enjoin the doing of that which is good and forbid the doing of that which is wrong with a kind of hatred, because they consider them to be acting as retardants in the process of the advent of the promised savior. If such people are not themselves sinners, they look upon sinners and the morally corrupt and degenerate with a kind of satisfaction, because they believe them to be laying the groundwork for the advent. In so far as this take on the advent is against reform and believes the increase in the corruption and degradation of society to be [necessary] preliminary elements and preludes to a sacred social explosion or revolution, should be considered to be a quasi-dialectical [i.e. Hegelian/ Marxist] ideology, with this difference: that in the dialectical ideology [of Marxism], the intensification of chaos is allowed and justified because it deepens the [social] schisms, thereby adding fuel to the fire of resistance; whereas this other false and ignorant view allows and justifies the increase in corruption and chaos for its own sake so that somehow the desired result will be obtained automatically. The result of this waiting posture can be nothing, but anguish and frustration and it has no positive results to show for itself; a person waiting with such a negative posture of expectancy is like one who is waiting for a beloved, and tries to occupy himself with some other task so as to keep his mind off his expectancy [instead of doing something to attract his beloved's attention or to bring about conditions which are conducive of his beloved's reciprocation of attention].

2. Constructive Awaiting

According to the Quran and to *hadīth* reports, the advent of the Mahdī ﷻ is a link in the chain of the struggle of the righteous against the forces of false and illegitimate authority, which will ultimately end in the victory of the righteous over the wicked. Now a given individual's having a share in the felicity of this victory obviously depends on his taking a position *in practice* on the side of the forces of the righteous.

The posture of awaiting that is proper and constructive is one where a person is not content with the status quo of tyranny and oppression, opposes it, and takes steps towards establishing a better and more just society. The basic indicator of an awaiting posture that is constructive is one that entails an optimistic outlook toward the future of humanity; a bright and happy and humane future in which corruption and evil will have been uprooted, and in which righteousness and God-fearing piety and justice and freedom and sincerity will triumph over the rule of violence and aggression, and over the rule of arrogant hegemonic forces the world over; in which maximal benefit will be had from the blessings of the earth; in which there will be perfect equality between men with respect to the distribution of wealth; and in which moral degeneracies such as fornication, unrestrained lust, usury, and the consumption of alcohol will have been eradicated.

This posture of awaiting is a dynamic one and one in which sustained actions of resistance are taken against the enemies of righteousness in order to enact reforms and establish justice. As such, this posture is very effective in bringing about God's ultimate promise, and is in fact a mutual and reciprocal response to that promise. It is like a situation where someone makes an appointment with another to meet him on such and such a date at such and such a time at a specific location, and so the other party must perforce go to that place at that time, for if he fails to do so, he will never make the appointment. Thus, it is not the case that his posture of expectancy and awaiting has no effect on the question of their meeting and that the two will meet irrespective of his posture. Rather, the posture of expectancy and awaiting is a kind of preparation for the meeting. Therefore, an awaiting that is authentic and true is realized when it spurs one to action and resistance against the enemies of truth and justice, and to action in the purification of one's own soul and of the reform of society at large.

The Longevity of the Life of the Imam al-Mahdī

One of the attributes and distinguishing characteristics of the universal savior in its Shīʻa conception is the longevity of his lifespan, which started with his birth (255 Lunar/ 867 CE) and continues to this day (about 1,150 years). Of course, there are those who consider such a long lifespan one that defines the laws of nature and of biological norms and therefore consider it to be impossible. But Shīʻa scholarship has responded to this objection from three basic approaches, each of which we shall proceed briefly to enumerate and explain:

1. The possibility of this phenomenon actually occurring

On the basis of numerous examples from the Word of God [i.e. the Quran; and the Bible too, incidentally], many prophets and saints were granted extremely long lifespans, of which we can point to the longevity of the lifespans of the prophet Noah ﷺ, the prophet Jesus [who is alive and whose return is expected by Muslims and Christians alike], of his Eminence Loqmān[13], and so on. Thus, if there is historical precedent for the longevity of the lifespan of such prophets and saints, then there is no reason to deny such a possibility in the case of the Imam al-Mahdī ﷺ.

2. The possibility of this phenomenon from a scientific vantage

It is possible to think of such an extended lifespan as a naturally occurring phenomenon. To wit: scientists are constantly attempting to find ways of prolonging man's lifespan with the tools and possibilities presently available to them. And while it is true that they have not met with any spectacular successes, nevertheless, their efforts in trying to achieve such successes speak loudly to their belief that such achievements *are* indeed in the realm of possibility.

3. The possibility of this phenomenon from a logical vantage

Even if we hold the position that the longevity of the lifespan of the Mahdī ﷺ is a breach of the laws of nature and that the issue of this breach is not resolved given the application of the latest technological achievements to the human body, all of this should still not prevent us from believing in the possibility of such an occurrence, because many of the great changes which have

---

[13] A Quranic character after whom the thirty-first *sūra* (chapter) of the Quran is named. Some consider him to be a prophet, but the Quran is silent on this point.

occurred in the history of different life forms, be they plant or animal, are abnormal changes. For example, the case of the first embryonic lifeform which appeared on Earth, or that of the first time a sign of life appeared on Earth cannot be a case which conformed to the laws of nature, and the latest advances in the life-sciences has yet to be able to explain the why or how of the quantum leap of the first appearance of embryonic lifeforms on Earth. Or to take the case of revelation itself: while there is no doubt that it is a supra-natural phenomenon, at the same time it has occurred time and again in the case of numerous divinely-inspired prophets, and is considered to be an obvious and given fact within the communities of faith throughout the world.

It is thus clear that extraordinarily long lifespans do not fall in the realm of logical impossibilities and are indeed logically possible. And in so far as the longevity of the life of his Eminence the Mahdī ؑ is considered to be a tenet of the faith within Twelver Shī'a Islam, and as there are many scriptural proofs available in support of this fact, we can conclude that his Eminence the Mahdī ﷻ has indeed been granted a lifespan of extra-ordinarily long duration.

4 Preludes to and Signs of the Advent

The manifestation of not a single phenomenon is a result of chance and happenstance, and stands in need of preparation and preliminary groundwork, and is bound by the laws of cause and effect. On this basis, then, the advent of the universal savior, as the most important event in the perfection of human history, is no exception to the laws which govern the world of existence, and stands in need of preparation and preliminary groundwork which, once in place, will bring about his advent.

We can point to reform processes and insurrectionary uprisings as instances of such preparatory groundwork. Gradual reforms come to the aid of those working for lasting peace through social justice against the forces of reaction, speeding the pace of historical change in their favor. Therefore, the pace of the progressive development of history and the coming of the universal savior is hastened with every reformatory measure, no matter how small in its impact it might be.

We can point to the coming into being of persons who have gradually approximated if not having attained to their own perfections in terms of their achievements in morality and the ideals of the humanities among the other preludes to the coming of the savior, meaning the coming into being of persons who have gotten closer to the ideal human and [are thus able better to envision] the ideal society. These are instances and cases in point of a group of elite persons which have been referred to in *hadīth* reports, who will join the Mahdī ﷻ immediately upon his manifestation on the physical plane. This group is composed of the most valuable of persons in terms of their faith, and in terms of their standing guard at night and day over the forces of righteousness; they have seen their training in the midst of tyranny and in the height of corruption and oppression, and are ready and busily engaged in laying the preparatory groundwork for the advent of the Mahdī ﷻ and his insurrectionary uprising. Thus, the presence of such valuable people is a necessity of the progressive developmental process of history and the coming of the universal savior. This transcendent goal will not be achieved absent such truth-seeking people. It is therefore everyone's religious duty to join these spiritual adepts,[14] to struggle for the manifestation of absolute good, and to fight against the obstacles in the path of the advent.

Now in the meantime, some people who have no expertise in and are not even familiar with the basic literature of the deep concept of Mahdism but who are operating under the influence of Marxist[15] ideology, and who have incorrect interpretations of certain *hadīth* reports, have taken the position that an increase in iniquity and oppression and corruption lays the foundations for the advent of the savior and hastens his manifestation.

From their perspective, any sort of sin or iniquity or prejudice etc. is the best means to hastening the advent of the savior because they lay the groundwork for the greater good, and that those who engage in these acts must be encouraged! As opposed to these, the work of the righteous who work to reform the ills of society and who enjoin the doing of that which is good and forbid the doing of that which is wrong is considered to be without merit because they are delaying the advent. This idea is the result of false interpretations of certain *hadīth* reports, to which we can respond as follows:

---

[14] Probable reference to Imam Khomeini and his movement.
[15] The contemporary equivalent would perhaps be pacifist and other pluralist ideologies.

1. The *hadīth* reports which are the basis of these beliefs speak of the abundance of oppression and corruption, and not of the abundance of oppressors and of the corrupt. For example, in a *hadīth* report of Imam Ja'far as-Sādeq ﷺ, he states, "This affair [the advent] will not occur until each of the wretched and the righteous reach the ultimate end of their respective deeds." What is being stated is that each of the members of the group of the righteous and the wretched attain to the ultimate end of their respective deeds, and not that there will no longer be anyone present from among the group of the righteous, and that only the wretched will be present to reach the ultimate end of their wretched deeds. Thus, while it is true that the wretched unbelievers will indeed attain to the ultimate depths of their wickedness, the true believers too will attain to the peaks of their own perfections so that they can aid the Imam; and this means that one must not countenance sin in oneself or in others because such a posture hinders the process of the perfection of humanity. In addition to this, there must exist people for whose cause the Imam's advent is intended to aid and make victorious; so, to whose cause will the Imam come to fight for if everyone has become corrupt and degenerate?

2. While humanity is heading for desolation, it is also heading toward greater order. Thus, abandoning one's religious duties[16] goes against a categorical ordinance of Islam, for if the truth of the matter were other than this, Islam would have ordained

---

[16] "Enjoining the doing of that which is good and forbidding the doing of that which is wrong" is a religious duty in Islam.

people to act differently in that particular period and to commit what was previously considered to be illicit, and to abandon that which was previously considered to be obligatory. Therefore, there is full consensus in both Shīʿa and Sunnī scholarship that in the period of awaiting the advent of the Mahdī ﷻ, none of the individual or social obligations of the religion may be abandoned or annulled.

3. Another false meme which has been put forward from certain quarters is that based on *hadīth* reports, no insurrectionary movement prior to the advent of the Mahdī ﷻ has any legitimacy and are false and represent illegitimate authority (*tāghūt*).[17] The *hadīth* report in question is the following:

> Any standard raised [in insurrection] before the rise of the Mahdī ﷻ is the standard of illegitimate authority (*tāghūt*).

In addition to the weakness of [the chain of custody in] the provenance title (*sanad*)[18] of these types of reports, as well as their content being contradicted by the principles of the sacred law of Islam, it can be said that the legitimacy and sacrality of social struggle does not revolve around the question of whether an individual or national right has or has not been violated. That which legitimates social struggle is a situation where in a given right is endangered, especially if this right is one which belongs

---

[17] See footnote #8 on page 39.
[18] Usually translated as "chain of transmission".

to the brotherhood of man at large. What legitimates the struggle for the rights of the downtrodden and for the maintenance of the integral social vision of Islam (*towhīd*)[19] is because these are the greatest assets of humanity. Therefore, gradual reforms, social struggle and insurrectionary uprisings against tyranny and injustice are by no means to be condemned as illegitimate; neither are their primary dynamics the conflicts [posited by the Hegelian dialectic], nor is it true that history's course runs from one negation to another in the fashion of a [Marxist] revolution of negation, for gradual reforms to thereby hinder the tendency of such revolutionary explosions thereby thwarting the supposed developmental progress of history. Rather, the insurrectionary movement of his Eminence the Mahdī ﷻ is naught but a movement of reform, and can in fact be considered to be the final and perfecting capstone capping all previous struggles for reform. Finally, gradual reforms, social struggle and insurrectionary uprisings against tyranny and injustice do not go against the basic Quranic principles expressed in the following verses:

إِنَّ اللَّهَ لَا يُغَيِّرُ مَا بِقَوْمٍ حَتَّىٰ يُغَيِّرُوا مَا بِأَنْفُسِهِمْ

[13:11] Verily, God ﷻ does not change men's condition unless they change their own condition.

And,

الَّذِينَ كَفَرُوا وَصَدُّوا عَن سَبِيلِ اللَّهِ أَضَلَّ أَعْمَالَهُمْ

---

[19] See footnote #5 on page 28.

[47:1] As for those who are bent on denying the truth and on barring [others] from the path of God ﷻ - all their [good] deeds will He let go to waste.

Thus, we can conclude that movements of social reform are a service which ultimately hastens that promised phenomenon of universal social reform of which the world is in wait.

If we look at the issue from the vantage of the *hadīth* reports corpus, we see that a series of insurrections and uprisings occur on the part of the righteous as preludes to the advent and uprising of the Imam himself. The uprising of "the Yamānī" is one such example, which itself does not occur without the preparatory groundwork being in place. In some *hadīth* reports there is even talk of a government of the righteous which is sustained until the uprising of the Mahdī ﷻ, such that a number of Shīʿa scholars had favorable views of their contemporaneous Shīʿa governments, allowing for the possibility that the respective governments might indeed be the 'government of the righteous' referred to in these reports. Thus, movements of social reform and insurrections for social justice which occur prior to the advent of the universal savior, far from being rejected as illegitimate, are to be welcomed and actively engaged in as they provide the necessary groundwork for His Eminence's advent.

Signs of the Advent

The preconditions for the realization of a given phenomenon differ from its signs; preconditions are necessary prerequisites and are inseparable from the phenomenon, which cannot and will not be realized until its preconditions are met. But the signs of a phenomenon simply herald the occurrence or the proximity of the occurrence of the phenomenon, and do not play a role in its realization, such that it is possible for the phenomenon to be realized without its signs being manifested.

This having been said, there are two types of signs mentioned in connection with the advent of the Mahdī. One group of such signs are described as being categorical in the *hadīth* report corpus, in the sense that their occurrence is not conditioned on anything and in the sense therefore that these signs *must* take place prior to the advent. Among these categorical signs are the Cry from the Heavens, the Rise of the Sofyānid, the Sinking of [the land of] Baydā[20] [into the Earth], the Rise of the Yamānid, and the insurrection of the *an-Nafs az-Zakīya* (the Purified Soul). The enumeration of these categorical signs is based on the *hadīth* report of Imam Ja'far as-Sādeq's, in which he states the following:

These five things are signs of the uprising of the One who will Arise [in insurrection to establish justice] (*al-Qāem*): the Cry from the Heavens, the Rise of the Sofyānid, the Sinking of [the

---

[20] Baydā: a desert valley located between Mecca and Medīna where the army of the Sofyānid is prophesied to be swallowed up by the earth.

land of] Baydā [into the Earth], the Rise of the Yamānid, and the murder of the Pure Soul (*an-Nafs az-Zakīya*).

The other group of the signs of the advent are the uncategorical signs, whose realization appears in the prophetic *hadīth* reports, but whose nature and scope is unspecified or uncertain. These include the following:

Before the advent of the Mahdī, there will be an unprecedented level of chaos, together with extremely terrible battles in an unprecedentedly dangerous war, which is said to stand upright and to show its teeth like a wild beast of prey. It is also said that troublemakers and firebrands will appear as never before. Thus, the advent of the universal savior will occur after the coming of times of great difficulty, insecurity, and war, for lightning strikes in the darkness of night.

5 The Uprising

According to our religious teachings, the insurrectionary movement and uprising of the Imam al-Mahdī ﷻ is an uprising for the reformation of society which will realize the transcendent goals and high ideals of humanity, thereby saving a humanity which had hitherto been subjugated and oppressed under various forms of subjugation and oppression, as well as being imprisoned by widespread ignorance, consummating mankind's felicity in this world and his salvation in the hereafter.

Any struggle and sacred insurrectionary movement has various attributes, and all of these characteristics appear in their perfected form in the insurrectionary movement and uprising of the Imam al-Mahdī ﷻ. These attributes include:

1. The ultimate cause of the movement is not of a private or individual nature, but is rather of a more general nature and stands for the establishment of social justice, human ideals, and for the implementation of the *towhīdic*[21] vision, all of which give the cause popular acceptance and support.

2. The uprising must be informed with the highest possible vision [of its objectives]. This important consideration will be fulfilled with the most visionary and politically conscious leaders within the movement of the Mahdī ﷻ.

3. The uprising of the Mahdī ﷻ is like a bolt of lightning which strikes in the darkest of nights, and a cry in the silence, and a motion in the midst of absolute stillness, in a condition where all attempts at reform are suppressed and crushed absolutely, and the atmosphere of political repression has resulted in a state of hopelessness and despair… out of which the Mahdī ﷻ will appear of a sudden. The Mahdī will appear at a time when tyranny and oppression have taken over the entire globe and when there is no longer any hope for the coming of a savior. As it also appears in prophecies of the Prophet ﷺ, [wherein it is

---

[21] See footnote #5 on page 28.

stated that] when the world reaches a stage when humanity is at risk of self-destruction and annihilation, God ﷻ will save humanity by means of a single person.

The advent of the savior can be likened to a fruit which must go through its various stages of development before it is ripe for the picking. Thus, the world must have reached a point where it is ready for and have the capacity to accept the savior before he appears. Although on one hand tyranny and inequity and corruption and oppression are increased, but on the other hand, there will appear righteous followers of the Mahdī who are pious and God-fearing and who struggle for bringing about the uprising and who join the wrathful uprising of the Imam at the time of the advent by renewing and deepening their vows with him.

It bears mentioning that the movement of humanity toward the advent is an inward circular motion like the contours of the shell of a snail, such that the advent will not occur until humanity reaches a dead-end. Therefore, there will always be frustration in the world, but this frustration will be followed by a new order, and this new order will turn to another frustration, but a frustration of a higher order, not of a lower one. In a similar fashion humanity will revolve in an upward circular motion until the highest level of frustration and distress is reached and the stage of the manifestation of the savior is at hand. Thus, while we are progressing toward the manifestation of the savior, we are heading toward greater frustration and distress, but of a higher level, such that we hear it said by intellectuals the world over that the only way to solve the problems facing humanity is the formation of a unitary world government, whereas such an idea would never have occurred to mankind before.

The Necessity of the Advent

Some are of the opinion that this is the era of scientific knowledge and that the ideal society has [already] been established with the help of the power of the human intellect and that man is not threatened by any danger. In the opinion of those who hold such a view, the main danger facing humanity is ignorance, because it is ignorance, in their view, that brings about the conditions for the annihilation of humanity and causes imbalances to enter the general order. But today – the thinking goes – where the light of science has lit the entire world, humanity is not threatened by any danger, making the advent of a savior from non-existent threats superfluous.

But the truth is that humanity's waywardness is not rooted simply in ignorance. Rather, the source for most of the problems of humanity is untamed urges and uncontrolled desires and socially damaging proclivities such as anger, aggression, carnal lust, greed, blind ambition, selfishness, and so on. These urges and desires, when not properly controlled, can even put the fruits of science and technology at their service and carry man to the brink of destruction. As can be seen clearly, in this day and age, untamed human urges and desires have reached a depth of madness that is even lower than its previous lows, where even science and technology have been turned into instruments that are at the service of these base desires. Therefore, scientific advances do not make a whit of difference in taming and reducing these socially destructive urges and have failed to reduce the material and base desires of man or to epiphanize the transcendental values in him.

Given this, the position that man is not threatened by any danger and that he has reached the peak of his development and that there is no need for the advent of any savior is an unexamined stance and should be rejected; and it is meet and proper that God's promise be realized in the advent of a savior to save humanity from the social and ethical problems that it faces. According to this explanation, then, it would seem that some of the reasons for the necessity of the savior are indeed indispensable.

1. The Response to the Innate Needs of Man

There is no doubt that planted within man are the seeds to a series of propensities and predispositions which must be guided for them to reach their perfected stage. Therefore, man is not like an empty vessel which is filled from without by external influences, nor is he like a raw material that is shaped into an industrial product by the blind forces of the means of production.

One of the most important dispositions of man's innate nature is his predisposition to seeking justice and to seeking his own perfection; at the same time, humanity has been frustrated throughout its history from achieving perfection and justice in any sense that can be considered to be complete. Thus, the innate driving force that recognizes the social order as it is in reality and at the same time envisages the ideal society as it should be, feels the disconnect between the two; and this ever-present disconnect acts as a mechanism that continually militates people to actions that attempt to bridge this gap, for the cause of which great hardships have been faced and at whose alter innumerable people have been sacrificed. The ministry of the prophets through the ages has also been to move people and nations in this same direction (which is demanded by their primordial and innate dispositions). The teachings of revealed scripture tell us that the path which this inward dynamic of our innate predisposition leads us to is ineluctable, and it is one which humanity as a whole will, after taking some wrong left and right turns, eventually settle down on, and will ultimately reach its perfection with the aid of the advent of the universal savior, thanks to the dignity and grace of the creator's creation.

2. The Necessity of the Triumph of Good over Evil

Before we proceed to an analysis of the reasons for this necessity, it behooves us first to explicate three preliminary concepts before introducing the actual reason.

1. That which in philosophical terminology is referred to as the natural order and the laws of cause and effect is referred to as the divine way or tradition [in the colloquial parlance of Islam], and this has three characteristics: being universal and unchanging, being divine[ly originated], and not being mutually exclusive with respect to man's freedom of will and action.

The teachings of revealed scripture tell us that the law of cause and effect is the ineluctable law with which the world is governed and is in effect in both the material and non-material domains. Therefore, the movement of the Mahdī ﷻ and his insurrection are no exception to this rule and fall under the aegis of these ineluctable laws. The Quran also definitively rejects the notion that the fate of history is determined by aimless chaotic forces and stipulates the unchanging nature of God's way in His ruling over peoples of the past:

فَهَلْ يَنظُرُونَ إِلَّا سُنَّتَ الْأَوَّلِينَ ۚ فَلَن تَجِدَ لِسُنَّتِ اللَّهِ تَبْدِيلًا ۖ وَلَن تَجِدَ لِسُنَّتِ اللَّهِ تَحْوِيلًا

[35:43] Do they expect anything other than [God's] way with those who lived before. No change wilt thou ever find in God's way; yea, no deviation wilt thou ever find in God's way!

But the traditions which govern the fates of nations are in fact a series of reactions to action, and specific reactions lie in the train of specific social actions, so that while history is governed by the ineluctable law of cause and effect, man's freedom of will and action is preserved, enabling people to change their destinies for the better or for the worse. As Almighty God ﷻ has stated:

نَّ اللَّهَ لَا يُغَيِّرُ مَا بِقَوْمٍ حَتَّىٰ يُغَيِّرُوا مَا بِأَنفُسِهِمْ

[13:11] Verily, God ﷻ does not change men's condition unless they change their own condition.

2. One of the characteristics of man is the inner tension between his downwardly tending urges and desires (which have no aim other than those concerning his own individual interests), and propensities which tend to elevate his spirit and whose dynamic is to transcend the limits of his individuality and to encompass the interests of the entirety of humanity. This primordial inner struggle of man which the ancients characterized as the struggle between the passions and reason inevitably turns into a conflict between two groups of men: those who are on a higher stage of their progressive development and perfection and who have attained to a certain amount of spiritual freedom, and those who are retrogressive and bound to their baser instincts.

Thus, from time immemorial, there has always been a battle between the partisans of righteousness whose leaders are of the ranks of the prophets Abraham ﷺ, Moses ﷺ, and Jesus ﷺ; and the partisans of false consciousness and of an iniquitous social order (*al-bātel*) whose leaders are of the ranks of Nimrod, Pharaoh, and the Jewish moneychangers which Jesus ﷺ drove out of the Temple [according to Matthew 21:12]. In these battles, the forces of righteousness have at times been victorious over the forces of iniquity, and at times it has been the other way around, but at all events, these victories and defeats have been dependent on a series of socio-economic and political causes.

3. The teachings of revealed scripture tell us that in the order of being, the world is founded upon truth, and falsehood is vanquished by truth, as witnessed by this noble verse:

$$\text{بَلْ نَقْذِفُ بِالْحَقِّ عَلَى الْبَاطِلِ فَيَدْمَغُهُ فَإِذَا هُوَ زَاهِقٌ ۚ وَلَكُمُ الْوَيْلُ مِمَّا تَصِفُونَ}$$

[21:18] Nay, but [by the very act of creation] We hurl the truth against falsehood, and it crushes the latter: and lo! It withers away. But woe unto you for the [false] things you ascribe [to Us and to the purpose of Creation].

This verse gives expression to the verity that falsehood cannot stand against truth forever, and while it might superficially triumph over truth and cloak it temporarily, it will be uprooted when truth goes up against it. So, this is the fashion in which falsehood is manifested in human society, and those who lack a sufficient depth of discernment look to the superficial reality and, ignoring the deeper reality at play, attribute ontic realities to falsehood over and above truth, whereas the order of truth is that which is real and that which has an ontological reality. Like the waves under the froth of the ocean, truth is in motion and moves society forward, leaving falsehood behind as a backwash or wastewater which owes its existence to truth.

Thus, falsehood's existence obtains on a superficial and experiential plane and does not obtain on a rational-analytical plane, and will ultimately be vanquished by truth.

We can conclude that while it is true that throughout the course of human history the conflict between truth and falsehood has always existed, nonetheless, the ultimate victory of truth over falsehood is a tradition of the divine, and the developmental progress of humanity proceeds toward freedom from material nature, economic indigence, and individual interests toward social interests, God-fearing piety, and religiosity, and the will of the more advanced human being is gradually freed from its bondage to the demands of his material environment and his animalistic and base desires as a result of his cultural development and his subsequent inclination to progressive ideologies. Now this victory will not take place absent the advent of a universal savior, and according to revelation, the insurrection of the Imam al-Mahdī ﷻ will be realized as the final link in the chain of the battles of the forces of righteousness over those of falsehood, after which the final victory of truth over falsehood shall be accomplished:

$$وَنُرِيدُ أَن نَّمُنَّ عَلَى الَّذِينَ اسْتُضْعِفُوا فِي الْأَرْضِ وَنَجْعَلَهُمْ أَئِمَّةً وَنَجْعَلَهُمُ الْوَارِثِينَ$$

[28:5] But it was Our will to bestow Our favor upon those [very people] who were [hitherto] deemed [so] utterly low in the land, and to make them forerunners in faith, and to make them heirs [to Pharaoh's wealth and glory].

3. Universal Unity

[The applicability of] Islam's ordinances are not limited to geographical or tribal or national boundaries; these ordinances have been ordained with a universal government in mind.

On one hand, the world is headed in the direction of a unitary government based on the world's needs, and of individual and collective exigencies. On the other, the current capabilities of man for the creation of such unity in government are insufficient, as mankind is what he is, and he is in danger of self-annihilation, as Lord Russell has stated most forcefully. And so mankind is moving toward a dead-end which will either result in his self-destruction or in the eventuality of his being granted a savior from the world of the unseen. Because there can be no doubt in the wisdom and grace of Almighty God, there can equally be no doubt that He will indeed save us from destruction at our own hands, which salvation will occur, so revelation tells us, at the hands of the promised and awaited universal savior or the Imam al-Mahdī.

The Advent and the Question of Free Will

The teachings of revealed scripture tell us that the primordial inner struggle of man which the ancients characterized as the struggle between the passions and reason will inevitably turn into a conflict between two groups of people: those who are on a higher stage of their progressive development and perfection and who have attained to a certain amount of spiritual freedom, and those who are retrogressive and bound to their baser instincts. The struggle between truth and falsehood which continues even to this day will ultimately result in the victory of the forces of truth over those of falsehood. The final triumph of the forces of righteousness will be the crowning act of history's developmental progress and perfection, realizing the ineluctable will of God.

However, the question presents itself as to the extent of the impact, if any, of man's freedom of will on this process. There are two positions that have been taken in response to this question.

The first position takes the view that it is only God's will which has any effect on the advent of the universal savior, and in so far as this advent is something that has been promised to mankind by God, the advent will take place whenever He wills it without any interference whatever from any human agency. According to this view, then, changes brought about in history by human agencies are not operative as criteria for the realization of the advent.

The second position, which is preferred, takes the view that in addition to God's will, human agencies are also effectual in the realization of the advent.

In reality, while it is true that history's march has been and is one of progressive development, and that mankind is generally marching toward its perfection, that nonetheless, considering the fact that the main agencies of historical change are human and that humans are free and have agency, and are extremely effectual with respect to their own future destiny (which they affect freely and consciously)... all this is to say that man is capable of freely and consciously choosing the path which his future is to take. He can choose a good future for himself, or a bad one. The world in which man finds himself is governed by the laws of cause and effect, and man is free and empowered to cause things to change by making social changes thereby setting the laws of cause and effect into motion and soliciting equal and opposite reactions from his natural environment. This is why the gradual reform of society has been stipulated, and why it is pointed out that the gradual changes and reforms which are brought about by means of human will and action are, in their own right, aids in the struggle between those who are on a higher stage of their progressive development and perfection and who have attained to a certain amount of spiritual freedom, against those who are retrogressive and bound to their baser instincts, and accelerates the pace of change in favor of the march of the righteous, and thereby contributes to the final perfection of history and the advent of the universal savior.

The Timing of the Advent

Some are of the opinion that the time of the advent can be determined given some of its non-categorical[22] signs, but the truth of the matter is that the timing of the advent, like the timing of the Day of Resurrection itself, is one of the most mysterious of worldly affairs for which a fixed time not only has not been prophesied either by the Prophet himself ﷺ, or by any of the Immaculate Imams ؑ, but rather, they have said that claimants who claim to be able to foretell its time should be controverted.

The Advent of the Savior and Assistance from al-Ghayb (the world beyond the ken of ordinary human perception)

Some believe that talk of the world of *al-ghayb* (usually translated as 'the unseen') and talk of the reality of supernatural assistance from the world beyond the ken of ordinary human perception and

---

[22] See the section 'Signs of the Advent' in Chapter Four.

its influence on our world and the lives of human beings in the era of scientific knowledge is nothing but superstition. According to what revelation teaches us, this phenomenal world of ours is ordered from and is dependent upon another world, and the archetypes or original specimens of things that appear in this world exist in a world beyond this one, and provide the existential basis of and spiritual scaffolding for their worldly analogues or simulacra. Our sacred teachings even tell us that every aspect of our private and social lives is suffused with help from the beyond. This divine succor and aid manifests itself at times by the bringing about of the conditions necessary for our success, and at other times appear in the form of inspirational guidance, spiritual, emotional, and mental breakthroughs, and the like.

Similarly, great prophets and *owlīā*[23] have appeared throughout all of human history like an invisible hand from the beyond and have saved humanity from catastrophes and disasters. The presence of these men has been like a rain that comes down on a parched desert. Similarly, the appearance of the universal savior can be likened to an invisible hand which emerges from the sleeve of dawn at the end of a dark night to save mankind from annihilation. Although the world is currently at the precipice of a dangerous turn in the road, God ﷻ will send a savior to humanity, just as He has done so on numerous occasions in the past (although on a smaller scale) when humanity was at a dangerous turn, and the magnanimity of His aid and grace will

---

[23] Those who have spiritual proximity to God; sometimes translated as 'saints'.

be of such an extent as to astound sober minds, and the order that will be established as the trophy of the advent will reign over the world entire.

6 The Just Order of Post-Adventist Society and the Attributes of the Post-Adventist Era

The study of history tells us that most people continually think of an ideal society free from iniquity and oppression in which they can live in perfect peace and security. Therefore, there has always been a struggle to reach such a goal, and these struggles have achieved certain gains. A number of thinkers such as Plato, Fārābī, Thomas Moor, Francis Bacon, and Augustine have attempted to present some of the ancient human ideals of "the virtuous city" which are achievable in practice in their political thought and writings, attempting to provide them with the solid footing of rational proofs; but there are differences between the ideal cities of these thinkers in terms of their qualities and attributes and ultimate purposes. For example, Plato and Fārābī focused their thought on the point that the ruler of the ideal city must necessarily be a philosopher or the "philosopher-king", positing that the world will attain to felicity when its rulers are philosophers and its philosophers are rulers, and as long as philosophers form one class and rulers form another, the world will not attain to felicity. Augustine, on the other hand, believed that the ruler of the ideal city should be a religious leader.

A Critique of the Theorizing for the Ideal City

The origins of the thoughts positing the Ideal City undoubtedly originate in the human condition, and many are of the opinion that the dominant motivation for positing the theory of an ideal city are personal and individual in nature; and this is because if one looks at the personal lives of those who have put such theories forward, we witness their hopes of being freed from their current condition and of attaining to a better one. Thus, theories whose origins and motivations are intertwined with human conditions and considerations cannot, by their very nature, be immune to these environmental factors and influences. To go back to the example we provided of Plato and Fārābī who based their theories on the competence of individuals (and that the ruler of the ideal city must necessarily be a philosopher), and focused and expended all of their intellectual energies on the question as to the kind of attributes such a leader must have, and so on; but Plato and Fārābī did not pay any attention to crucial questions such as how such a society is to be brought about, how it is to be ordered, under what systemic conditions and regulations are such "philosopher-kings" to reign, or the question of the vast influence that social organizations and systems have on the thoughts and actions and emotional and spiritual states of individuals, including that of the individual who is to rule as philosopher-king. This point has also been neglected that in a sound political order, scofflaws and delinquents have lesser opportunities and capabilities for trespassing the law, and conversely, in political orders which are unsound, or which have been corrupted, righteous individuals have lesser opportunities and capabilities for practicing their lawful intentions. The dynamic tends toward dragging the righteous if not toward the wicked, then at least to a grey middle-ground between the two poles. As some have stated, Plato's placing the question of the leadership of society front and center in the issue of political theory committed a dangerous and lasting error in the field of political philosophy; and that the basic questions relating to political theory are better framed in terms of how we can organize society in such a way as to preclude bad rulers from attaining to power, and how we are able to minimize the impact of such people on society in the event that they do in fact attain to power.

The truth is that the impact and thus significance of righteous leaders is limited to the way in which they look upon the issues involved in the reform of the social organizations within the societies which they head. Additionally, that righteous leaders whose basic ideas about how society is to be managed and reformed is similar to or not much different than that of those who are not competent for the task (and whose merits over the latter are limited to their ethical conduct and other such attributes) will not be effective as leaders who bring about significant and lasting social change.

We can thus point out that the kinds of leaders who Plato and Fārābī have had in mind are those who have full control over society and its structural elements and not ones who are controlled by them or are its unwitting victims.

The structural elements of a given society and the way in which its sub-formations are organized and administered can be likened to the avenues, streets and alleys of a city, and how these interface with the citizens and modes of transportation which course through that city; in the sense that these modes of transportation and the citizenry of a given city have no choice but to negotiate the twists and turns of the roads and byways of the city as they have been constructed. The maximum amount of freedom of movement which people have in such situations is the choice as to which streets to take to arrive at their destination, some of which might be more scenic and take longer to arrive at a given destination, and others of which might be shorter and are, say, more congested. If we assume that the city in question has developed incrementally and without any forethought or based on the principles of city planning, its denizens are condemned to conform the comings and goings of their lives to the conditions which confront them. And even though this will of course be difficult and impose preventable hardships, once the city has developed in this way, there is not much that the leadership of that city can do to its transportation infrastructure, other than to ensure that the roads and structures which they have inherited as a *fait accompli* are properly maintained and remain serviceable, or in short, to make the best of a bad situation. Similarly, if we assume that righteous leaders are at the helm of organizations which are structurally deficient, the differential between their effectiveness and that of an incompetent leadership is no more than the choice of routes to a given destination in an unplanned city.

The Virtuous City of the Society of the Mahdī
Marxists who have a materialist view of man equate authority with power and brute force, and thus equate the absence of

oppression and the establishment of justice with the 'withering away' of the state and its authority. The truth is that the complexity of the social life of humanity and the administration of its complex web of relationships necessitates a widespread organization called government which is capable of taking on the leadership and decision-making responsibilities which social life demands in order to resolve conflicts and to ensure proper and equitable social transaction.

Imāmī or Twelver Shī'a scholarship has a realistic take on the notion of government, taking the view that legitimate authority is not the same thing as raw power and brute force, and that the most basic and most important element in man's attaining to his ideals is the formation of a government which is based on his religious tenets. Therefore, the government which is to be established by the Mahdī, like the imamate of Imam Ali ﷺ, will be a paragon of justice and the rule of law, whose leader will be an Immaculate Imam designated by Almighty God ﷻ who is not content simply to promulgate correct beliefs among the people, but takes the reins of power into his hands, and with the aid of righteous helpers and divine guidance, establishes the Virtuous City on earth, and eliminates insecurity, injustice, chaos and corruption from society, and delivers humanity to its ultimate ideals, the most important of which are the following:

1. The Establishment of Justice

From the vantage of Islamic scholarship, justice is a reality which comes about because of innate competences within man on one hand, and as a result of effort and struggle on the other. It consists of ensuring that any merit and right which anyone naturally has (as a result of a birthright), or has earned as a result of any effort or work on his part, and that these rights are given to each and every person. In contrast, inequity and oppression consist of withholding rights to which one is rightfully entitled. Discrimination is also another form of injustice, where two people are treated unequally under conditions that are otherwise equal.

That having been said, we turn again to the Marxists [and others] who claim that mankind cannot establish justice because neither can he be brought up and trained in such a way to where he desires justice from the inner depths of his being, nor can man's knowledge and reason be expanded and strengthened to the point where he sees his own interests and welfare as merging with the interests and prosperity of his fellow man and of society at large. However, from the Islamic perspective, the innate human desire for the establishment of justice is indeed an attainable objective, the seeds of which are implanted within man's being; but because man has not yet reached his perfection, justice eludes him; but if he is summoned to his true nature and attains to his perfection, he will prefer what is just for his community over his own individual and selfish interests.

To elaborate, we can say that mankind must pass through three distinct developmental stages: the stage of fables and fairytales or, in the words of the Quran, the era of ignorance (*jāhelīaʿ*); the era of knowledge which is combined with the reign of force and that of man's base desires; and the era wherein mankind is prepared for the acceptance of universal justice and the brotherhood of man.

In this third stage, with their reaching the stage of their perfection, people realize that all of the proclamations of human rights and human freedom and quests for justice of the past era were nothing but lies and hypocrisy, and that it is only the post-adventist era which is the era where human rights and freedoms will truly be established; because in addition to man's readiness for the acceptance of universal freedom, there will be an Immaculate Imam who is immune to error and sin who will be at the helm of humanity's ship of state.

1.1 Economic Justice

Economic justice is defined as sustainable economic growth, equity in the distribution of wealth, and the creation of the preconditions necessary for the welfare of individual members of society. In the Era of the Advent, which is the era where justice will be institutionalized in every aspect of human existence, every criterion and indicator of economic justice will be fulfilled, and any and all kinds of economic inequality and iniquity and discrimination and poverty will be uprooted:

- Equity in the distribution of wealth: equality and balance in economic welfare will be established between all mankind, just as the Most Noble Prophet ﷺ has stated: "[The Mahdī] will distribute wealth properly among people."

- Equity in social welfare: In the Era of the Advent, the maldistribution of wealth and other economic inequalities, and man's falling prey to poverty and indigence will be abolished, and everyone will be the beneficiary of the freedom from want. The Immaculate [Imams] state: "In the era of the Mahdī ﷻ, wealth will be plenteous, such that anyone who approaches the Mahdī ﷻ and asks him for financial assistance, will be given it immediately."

- Sustainable economic growth: Society's economic growth in the Era of the Advent, and the increase in production and the supply of goods is aided not just by the mastery of new technologies, but also by divine aid, which will come to the assistance of humanity and have a positive effect on the rate of economic growth. The Most Noble Prophet ﷺ stated: "The Mahdī ﷻ will arise in my community... and in his time, people will attain to such bounties the likes of which they have never experienced. The heavens will pour forth their bounties on the wicked and righteous alike, and the earth will not hold back any of its produce [from a single soul]."

Therefore, the earth will pour forth its bounties and its [full] capacities, and the keys to the secrets of nature will be at the disposal of the true believers, and there will be no secret [that will benefit mankind] whose veil will not be rended.

1b. Juridical Justice

In the Era of the Advent, the administration of justice will be based on the truth and what is truly just, and the Hall of Justice of the Imam al-Mahdī ﷻ will insist on justice being served for all alike, nothing more and nothing less, to the point that if somebody's right is held in someone else's clutches, his clutches will be pried apart and the right removed, as has been described by Imam Ja'far as-Sādeq ﷺ: "The world will not come to its end until a man from my family rises up [in insurrection for the establishment of justice and equity]. He will judge in the way in which David ﷺ judged. He will require evidence [to be presented], and will give everyone his due."

2. The Fulfillment of the Mission of the Prophets

According to the teachings of revealed scripture, the divinely-commissioned prophets have attempted to realize two ideals and objectives for humanity. The first is the establishment of the correct and proper relationship between man and God, moving man in the direction of the worship of God ﷻ as He should be worshipped in accordance with the principle of the unicity of God ﷻ (*towhīd*), which is summed up in the phrase *lā illāha illā Allāh* (there is no deity other than Allāh). The second objective is the establishment of the correct and proper relationship between man and his fellow man on the basis of justice, peace and security, brotherhood and brotherly love for and selfless service to one another, which is summed up in the following verse:

قَدْ أَرْسَلْنَا رُسُلَنَا بِالْبَيِّنَاتِ وَأَنزَلْنَا مَعَهُمُ الْكِتَابَ وَالْمِيزَانَ لِيَقُومَ النَّاسُ بِالْقِسْطِ

[57:25] Indeed, [even aforetime] did We send forth Our apostles with all evidence of [this] truth; and through them We bestowed revelation from on high, and [thus gave you] a balance [wherewith to weigh right and wrong], so that men might behave with equity.

Thus, becoming conscious of Almighty God 🕋 and establishing equity and justice and the transcendent human values in the realm of the social form the basis of the bringers of revealed wisdom, the second element of which, while a value in its own right, is considered a preliminary requisite to attaining to the first and primary objective. This notwithstanding, the principles and ideals of the divinely commissioned prophets (unto all of whom be God's peace) has not as yet been fully realized in the social life of humanity because their ministries have always faced a level of resistance which has precluded the complete realization of these ideals. But in the Era of the Advent, the developmental path of humanity and the transcendent social objectives of humanity will reach their fulfillment in the full light of the teachings of the divine religions, and the ministry of the *olu'l-azm*[24] apostles

---

[24] There are "124,000" prophets to which God 🕋 has spoken throughout the ages. Of these, approximately 300 have been apostles, i.e. those prophets who have been tasked with communicating God's will to mankind. In turn, of these 300, there have been five who have been

(those endowed with [a great] resolve) – who are the waystations on the developmental path of history, and the era of every prophet who is a bringer of a new dispensation is a stepping stone to the next higher stage – and especially the ministry of the Greatest Prophet ﷺ. And this progression will reach its ultimate stage in the Era of the Advent, which will be the culmination of the work of all of the past prophets, and humanity will at last become the beneficiary of the tree which the divinely-commissioned prophets through the ages have cultivated so diligently so that as to ensure that it should bear fruit. As Imam Ja'far as-Sādeq علیه السلام has stated:

> "At the time of the Advent of the Mahdī عجل الله تعالی فرجه الشریف, he will go to the *Masjed al-Harām* (the House of God ﷻ which houses the *ka'ba* in Mecca), and will face the *ka'ba* with his back to the Station of Abraham, make two cycles of the ritual devotions (*salā'*), and then say: 'O ye people! I am the reminder of Adam علیه السلام and the reminder of Abraham علیه السلام, and the reminder of Ishmael علیه السلام, and the reminder of Mohammad ﷺ.'"

As Imam Mohammad al-Bāqer علیه السلام has also stated:

---

given a Sacred Writ or "Book" and who have brought a new *sharī'a*ᵗ or Sacred Law and Dispensation to various peoples; namely: the prophets Noah, Abraham, Moses, Jesus and Mohammad, may the peace and blessings of God ﷻ be with them all. Mohammad ﷺ is the last of these five *olu'l-azm* apostles (literally meaning 'those endowed with a great resolve'), and was given the Qoran as his book and sacred writ.

[Upon his Advent,] the One who will Arise [in insurrection to establish justice] (*al-Qāem*) will be in Mecca and will say to the people, 'Let he who speaks of Adam ﷺ know that I am the inheritor of Adam ﷺ; Let he who speaks of Noah ﷺ know that I am the inheritor of Noah ﷺ; Let he who speaks of Abraham ﷺ know that I am the inheritor of Abraham ﷺ, and let he who speaks of Mohammad ﷺ know that I am the inheritor of Mohammad ﷺ. And let any who speak of any of the prophets ﷺ know that I am the inheritor and reminder [of the teachings of all] of the prophets ﷺ.

3. Religion in the Era of the Advent

In the Era of the Advent, the anthem of the worship of the One God ﷻ will be heard the world over, and with the vanquishing of the reign of false and illegitimate authority and of idolatry and heathenism, the religion of Islam will triumph over the entire world, and the divine message of revelation will have reached every ear, and God's promises to mankind will see their fulfillment, as stated in the following verse:

هُوَ الَّذِي أَرْسَلَ رَسُولَهُ بِالْهُدَىٰ وَدِينِ الْحَقِّ لِيُظْهِرَهُ عَلَى الدِّينِ كُلِّهِ وَلَوْ كَرِهَ الْمُشْرِكُونَ

[9:33] He it is who has sent forth His Apostle with the [task of spreading] guidance and the religion of truth, to the end that He may cause it to prevail over all religion, however hateful this may be to those who ascribe divinity to aught beside God ﷻ.

The interesting point to note is that certain *hadīth* reports state that at the time of the advent of the Lord of the Age[25] ﷻ, he will take certain actions which will prompt some to think that he has brought a dispensation or religion to humanity which is other than Islam. But the teachings of revealed scripture tell us that the truth is that Islam is an eternal religion (i.e. the efficacy and applicability of its dispensation and laws are eternal), and His Eminence the Lord of the Age ﷻ will not be bringing a new book and a new dispensation with him, but that during the length of the life of Islam to date, incorrect interpretations of the teachings of the Quran and of the noble Messenger of God ﷺ have added numerous extraneous accretions and innovations to Islam's laws and teachings, and many things that are ordained as mandatory have become prohibited (*monkerāt*), and vice versa. In this way, much of the truth of Islam has been covered up and is alien to many if not to most. When His Eminence the Lord of the Age ﷻ rises up [in insurrection for the establishment of justice and equity] and presents Islam as it truly is and executes its laws [as they were meant to be implemented], many will think that the religion which he has brought is not Islam but is a new religion; while the Lord of the Age ﷻ will be implementing Islam as it really is and should be, and will be revivified, executing the truths of Islam as they actually are.

---

[25] A title of the Imam al-Mahdī ﷺ.

4. The Perfection of Human Society

From the point of view of the Imamīya Shī'a, human history is a motion which passes in warps and woofs as it progresses toward its ideals and towards its ultimate perfection, which is a stage in the life of humanity which is perfected and without flaw and defect, and peace and security and justice and a state of general welfare for all suffuses the entire globe, and the life of humanity reaches its most exalted and perfected stage. This developmental stage encompasses much more than merely material progress and embraces man's spiritual, emotional, and social dimensions as well. These we shall expound upon in their own right in the sections which follow.

4.1. Intellectual Perfection

Today, people consider the modern era to be the era of science and reason and intellection and for it to be taking strides in the way of scientific advancements and technological achievements, with the presupposition that the power of his faculty of intellection will help man attain all of his needs and desires, However, the scientific and technological progress which man has made to date has not been able to achieve any of the basic ideals of humanity, such as peace and security, justice and equity, and the freedom from want and indigence; and this is because in this era, man's intellect (and "scientific" learning) has not had a proper understanding of what freedom truly is, and what it means truly to evolve to a higher stage of human development. This "progress" has in fact been at the service of baser desires, libidinal urges, unchecked ambition and material and selfish interests. When His Eminence the Lord of the Age ﷻ rises up [in insurrection for the establishment of justice and equity], he shall focus humanity's intellectual competencies in the right direction and guide them to their perfection, such that man's thought will be emancipated from the vicious downward spirals of man being controlled by his lusts and base desires, and he will be ruled by his perfected intellect. Therefore, the Era of the Advent is the era of the reign of reason, i.e. an era in which science is not bound by and put in the service of base desires and proclivities and is instead put in the service of religion and the implementation of the teachings of the Divine: "In that era, the goblet from which people drink morning and night is the goblet of wisdom and divine teachings... when His Eminence the Lord of the Age عَجَّلَ اللهُ تَعَالَى فَرَجَهُ الشَّرِيف will place his hand on the crown of people's heads and [miraculously] perfect the power of their reason."

4.2. Spiritual Perfection

The Era of the Advent is one where conditions are conducive for the growth of man's transcendental spiritual tendencies and the development of man's higher virtues, and where man is freed from the domination of social conditions, becoming more dependent on [implementing the tenets of his] faith, to the point that the hearts of God's devotees become filled with worship and devotion, the Islamic community is reformed, crime and sin diminish, and moral depravities such as fornication, the consumption of alcohol, usury, rancor, lying, betrayal, theft, etc. reach minimal levels, and man is ultimately freed from the chaos of his spiritual crisis and attains to his desired state.

4.3. The Perfection of Freedom

Freedom is a concept which can be summarized in three different categories: freedom from lower urges and desires; freedom from exploitation, and freedom from exploiting others.

In the Era of the Advent, with the breaking of the hold of the exploiters on the exploited on one hand, and the perfection of the human intellect and the subsequent flowering of his true and primordial nature, man will be witness to the peak of the perfection of his freedom in its true sense in all of the above domains.

5. Unicity and Integrality

Attaining to unicity [of purpose] and to integrality in the social order has been a human ideal, and many thinkers have tried to find ways of achieving this end. The historical process also reveals a dynamic which tends toward the unification and integration of societies and the merging and fusion of civilizations and cultures. The future of human society is a unitary perfected society in which all of the potential values of humanity are realized, and mankind will finally attain to its true perfection and felicity and authentic humanity. This will be such that the main causes of the division of mankind, meaning tribal, national, geographical and ideological and creedal differences will disappear and the unicity [of purpose] and the integrality in the social order will be achieved throughout the entire world under the auspices and absolute reign of Islam as it was truly meant to be, and the brotherhood of man will become universal.

6. The Dawn of the Life of Humanity

Without doubt, the life of humanity is dependent on his mental and intellectual and rational life; it is through these faculties that humanity becomes conscious and reaches the full flower of its growth. Thus, it is established in Islamic philosophy that science and the external world are interrelated such that the growth of science brings about a concomitant growth in [man's vision of the nature and magnitude of] the world, and [this outlook also gives rise to the truism that] 'he who is more conscious has a greater [magnitude of] soul'. And with the perfection of the intellect and the rational domain of man's existence, man attains to that aspect of his existence which is real, thus commencing a new era in his existence. And this is because many of the basic concerns and crises that man faces will have been uprooted, and man will attain to a favorable and desirable state.

7. Universal Peace and Security

Security is one of the most important blessings God has given us, and the most valuable asset a society can have; in the Era of the Advent, it is a quality which will become pervasive on the basis of man's primordial disposition (*fetra*), shedding the rays of its light on the just society of the Mahdī, as witnessed by the words of Imam Ali:

> When the One who will Arise [in insurrection to establish justice] (*al-Qāem*) rises up [in insurrection for the establishment of justice and equity], the skies will pour down rain as they are meant to pour

down rain on account of his *welāya'* (proximity to God; sovereignty) and the soundness of his lofty character (*adālat*), and the earth will spring forth its herbage and vegetation, and the hearts of God's bondsmen will be cleansed of all rancor, and peace will prevail between livestock and beasts of prey, such that a woman will be able to traverse on foot the distance between Iraq and ash-Shām (the Levant) without being molested, and wherever she steps shall be lush and green, and she will be able to display her ornaments and jewelry on her head without fear of being molested. Thus, if an old woman wants to journey from the east [end] of the world to its west [end], no one will disturb her. Even wolves and [other] beast of prey will live together in peace and security.[26]

The point to note is that the source of most insecurities is the absence of justice, which causes many to be deprived of their rights, leading some of them to act in an inappropriate manner [to make up for the transgressions of their rights], which actions in turn reduce the general security for all, so that when justice is established and prevails throughout the globe, security will also prevail in every street and township.

---

[26] Mohammad Bāqer Majlesī, *Behār ol-Anwār*, 10:104.

8. The Progress of Material and Industrial Society

The Era of the Advent is an era of basic changes in industry, such that technology and industry reach their respective zeniths, assisting mankind in attaining to prosperity and affluence.

Imam Ja'far as-Sādeq states:

> In the Era of the Advent, the true believer (*mo'min*) will be able to see his brother while he is in the east and his brother is in the west, and similarly, he who is in the west will be able to see those who are in the east.[27]

---

[27] Mohammad Bāqer Majlesī, *Behār ol-Anwār*, 52:391.

His Eminence, the Imām al-Mahdī
The Universal Savior of Humanity
By Abdol-Rahīm al-Mūsawī

Preface

The belief in the coming of a world savior and the establishment of a universal just order is not limited to the worldview of the revealed religions but is something that certain intellectual and philosophical traditions believe in as well. For example, the doctrine of the communists posits history as a clash or series of tensions (which are labelled alternatively as the 'theses' and 'antitheses' of history), and says that a promised day will arrive where these tensions shall cease to exist and peace and tranquility shall reign over the world.[28]

A number of prominent thinkers whose worldview is not religious also have this belief. For example, the famous British philosopher Bertrand Russell has said, "The world is waiting for a savior to unite it under a single cause and banner."[29]

---

[28] Mohammad Bāqer as-Sadr, *A Discussion Concerning the Mahdī*, p. 87.
[29] Quoted in Abdol-Redā Shahrestānī, The Awaited Mahdī and the Disabuse of Misunderstandings concerning Him, page 6.

The world-famous physicist Albert Einstein also has said, "The day is not far when peace and tranquility will be established on earth and people will live in peace and act with love and kindness toward each other."[30]

The much-decorated Irish playwright and critic G. Bernard Shaw addresses the need for the coming of a savior with a greater attention to detail, saying that "He is alive and endowed with a strong physical body and an extraordinary mind. He is a perfect man to whose example humanity can strive to reach. His lifespan will extend to approximately three hundred years, and he will be able to use the experiences which he has gained [from his long life]."[31]

The revealed religions all point to the certainty of the coming of a universal savior, and anyone who studies the sacred texts of these religions will see that the savior concerning whom glad tidings have been given in these texts refers to the same person that Shī'a Shī'a Islam believes in and who is referred to within that tradition as the Mahdī (the Guided One) and the Sāheb oz-Zamān (the Lord of the Age).

After having carried out in-depth research into the glad tidings concerning the universal savior provided in the Book of Isaiah, Qādī Sābātī concludes: "This text expressly states that he [the savior] is the Mahdī... The Imāmī [Twelver] Shī'a say that he is

---

[30] *Ibid*.
[31] Abbās Mahmūd ol-Aqqād, *Bernard Shaw*, pages 124-125.

Mohammad b. al-Hasan al-Askarī ﷺ who was born in the year 255 Lunar in Sāmarrā during the era of al-Moʿtamed, the Abbāsid caliph. His mother was named Narjes, the bondsmaiden of Hasan al-Askarī ﷺ. He became occulted for a year[32], then he reappeared, then became occulted again; and this [second occultation] is [what has come to be known as] the Greater Occultation, after which [absence] he will not return until God ﷻ wills it... I have mentioned the beliefs of the Shīʿa [concerning the coming of the Savior] insofar as they conform most closely to this text, and my objective has been to defend the community of [those who have attained to faith in the prophethood of] Mohammad ﷺ irrespective of sectarian considerations; I therefore have concluded that, that which the Shīʿa believe conforms most closely with the sacred Book [of Isaiah in the Old Testament]."[33]

Mohammad Reda Fakhroleslām, who was a Christian who converted to Islam and chose the Shīʿa rite for his practice, has likewise reached this same conclusion. He wrote an encyclopedic book in refutation of Judaism and Christianity called Anīs ol-Aʾlām wherein he investigated the various glad tidings that have been given concerning the coming of a universal savior and

---

[32] The historical truth of the matter is that the Lesser Occultation of the Imām al-Mahdī ﷺ took place for a period of 69 years after the death of his father, during which he maintained contact with his community by means of four Deputies, after which he went into the prolonged or Greater Occultaion.

[33] *Al-Barāhīas-as-Sābātīya*, quoted in Mīrzā Nūrī, *Kashf ol-Astār*, p. 84.

reached the conclusion that these were all in conformance with the Mahdī, the son of Hasan al-Askarī ﷺ."[34]

Anyone who studies the Bible carefully will discover that the attributes that appear in it concerning the universal savior about whom the Bible has provided glad tidings do not apply to anyone other than the Mahdī who is awaited by the Shī'a of the Ahl al-Bayt (the Members of the Household of the Prophet ﷺ); therefore, one who is not familiar with the beliefs of the Members of the Household of the Prophet ﷺ cannot attain to a proper understanding of the confirming indicators of the tidings provided in the Bible. As an example, an exegete of the Book of Revelation (or the Apocalypse of John as it is also called) has stated concerning verse 17:10, "The person concerning whose advent these prophecies give glad tidings has yet to be born, thus, the clear meaning [as to whom] these verses [refer] will become clear [at a time] in the future when the universal savior has appeared [on the scene]."[35]

A number of Sunni scholars have reached the same conclusion. For example, professor Saī'd Ayyūb has concluded that the prophecies of the Book of Revelation refer to the same person who the Imāmī (Twelver) Shī'a believe in and whose advent they are expecting. He writes, "In the sacred books of the prophets it is written that the Mahdī will be inerrant;" and comments, "I

---

[34] Mohammad Sādeqī, *Beshārat al-Ahdayn* (*Tidings of the Two Testaments*), page 232.
[35] *Ibid*, page 264.

attest that I have found the Mahdī as so described in the books of the ahl al-ketāb (the People of the Book; i.e. the Christians and Jews); and the People of the Book have studied the prophecies relating to the Mahdī, just as they had studied the prophecies concerning his ancestor [reference to the Prophet Mohammad ﷺ].

Revelations 12:1 refers to a woman who gives birth to twelve men. It then refers to another woman who is the woman who is to give birth to the last man in the series of twelve who are the issues from the loins of the first woman. In the passage from Revelations which follows, the dragon symbolizes the difficulties that the woman will face, standing before her and ready to devour the child she is to give birth to, which is an allegory of the dominant governing order being intent on killing the new-born child:

> [Revelations 12:3] And there appeared another wonder in heaven; and behold a great red dragon, having seven heads and ten horns, and seven crowns upon his heads. [Revelations 12:4] And his tail drew the third part of the stars of heaven, and did cast them to the earth: and the dragon stood before the woman which was ready to be delivered, for to devour her child as soon as it was born.

Revelations describes the birth of the child, and how he will be "caught up unto God":

[Revelations 12:5] And she brought forth a man child, who was to rule all nations with a rod of iron: and her child was caught up unto God, and to his throne. [Revelations 12:6] And the woman fled into the wilderness, where she hath a place prepared of God, that they should feed her there a thousand two hundred and threescore days.

In his commentary on the above verses, Barclay says that when the woman is surrounded by danger, God ﷻ protects the child by making him disappear from view. The disappearance of this child shall be 1,260 days – a period of time which is laden with significance and mystery among the Christians.[36]

Barclay continues his commentary concerning the progeny at large of the first woman: "The dragon, that is the Devil, on being cast out of heaven and descending to earth, attacked the woman who was the mother of the man child," as it also appears in Revelation 12:13: "And when the dragon saw that he was cast unto the earth, he persecuted the woman which brought forth the man child [who is destined to establish God's will on earth]."

---

[36] This duration is symbolic and cryptic. In the original Hebrew it appears as follows: "He will quickly disappear from the face of the serpent for a time, and times, and half a time;" cf. Mohammad Sādeqī, *Beshārat al-Ahdayn* (*Tidings of the Two Testaments*), page 263.

Professor Saī'd Ayyūb writes that "the above verses are descriptions of the Mahdī and correspond with the descriptions which the Twelver Shī'a believe concerning him."[37]

We therefore see that many different investigators and researchers have concluded that the tidings provided in the Bible point to the Mahdī whose descriptions correspond with the beliefs of, and to who is awaited by, the faithful of Shī'a Islam.

Given the fact that the beliefs of the Shī'a concerning Imām Mahdī ﷻ are relatively clear and that many detailed books have been written in which hadīth reports from Shī'a sources concerning the subject have been compiled, we shall proceed herein to survey hadīth reports which appear exclusively in the Sunni sources concerning Imām Mahdī ﷻ.

During the course of the review of these sources, what we are interested in resolving is the question as to whether or not these Sunni reports also discuss the details of the rank, station, attributes and character of the Imām al-Mahdī ﷻ; or if they simply point to the certainty of his advent at some future point in time.

---

[37] *al-Masīh ad-Dajjāl*, Saī'd Ayyūb, pages 379 – 380, where he brings evidence in confirmation of this thesis (quoted in *al-Mahdī al-Montazer fī'l-Fekr al-Islamīya*).

It should be evident that belief and the attaining to certainty in the advent of a universal savior cannot be useful or be in conformance with the demands of the Islamic mission without it being rooted in true knowledge concerning the character and attributes of such a savoir. This is because belief in an advent at some promised time in the future as an abstract principle divorced from faith and belief in Imām Mahdī ﷻ as a person is a corruption of the original concept which renders it useless. An analogy might be the case of one who believes in the obligation to perform the canonical devotions (*salā*) but who has no idea as to how these are to be performed, in which case such a belief would be useless. In this book, then, we shall review the understanding of Imām Mahdī ﷻ as it has reached us through the Sunni sources.

1 The Avowal of the Sunni Olamā to the Birth of Imām Mahdī

A large number of the Sunni olamā have avowed the birth of the Imām al-Mahdī ﷻ, and some have even prepared books wherein such admissions have been especially compiled. These avowals begin from the era of the Lesser Occultation (260 to 329 Lunar) and can be seen continually to the present day to the extent that it is as if the olamā are speaking with a concerted voice. Here we shall cite only a few examples of these avowals, and refer the reader to the detailed books on the subject for more comprehensive treatments.[38]

1. Eben Athīr al-Jazrī, Ezzeddīn (d. 630 Lunar).

In his *al-Kāmel fi't-Tārikh*, Eben Athīr writes under the events of the year 260: "In this year, the Ālid Abū-Mohammad al-Askarī ﷻ left the world. According to the Imāmī rite, he is one

---

[38] See, for example, Seyyed Qazwīnī, al-Imān as-Sahīh; Shaykh Mahdī Faqīh-Īmānī, al-Imām al-Mahdī fī Nahj ol-Balāgha; Tabrīzī, Man hūwa al-Mahdī; Yazdī al-Hāerī, Elzām an-Nāseb; Dakhīl, Mohammad Ali, al-Imām al-Mahdī; and Seyyed Thāmer al-'Amīdī, Defā' an al-Kāfī. In this last book, the avowals of 128 people of the Sunnite rite concerning the birth of Imām Mahdī ﷻ have been compiled and ordered in accordance with the century in which the person in question flourished. The first of these is Abū-Bakr b. Hārūn (d. 307 Lunar), who refers to the Mahdī's birth in his book al-Masnad which is available in manuscript form; and the last entry belongs to the contemporary scholar Yūnes Ahmad as-Sāmarrāī, who refers to the birth in his book Sāmarrā' fī Adab al-Qurān ath-Thāleth al-Hejrī, which was printed by the University of Baghdad in 1968 (cf. Defā' an al-Kāfī, 1:568-592).

of the Twelve Imāms and is the father of Mohammad, whom they believe to be the awaited Imām."[39]

2. Eben Khalkān (d. 681 Lunar).
Eben Khalkān writes in his Wafāt ol-A'yān, "Abol-Qāsem Mohammad b. Hasan al-Askari ﷺ b. Alī al-Hādī ﷺ b. Mohammad al-Jawād ﷺ, who we had mentioned earlier, is the Twelfth Imām of the Shī'a and is known as the Hojjaᵗ. He was born on the Friday of the middle of the month of Sha'bān in the year 255." Eben Khalkān then quotes from the Mayyāfāreqīn history of the historian and traveler Eben Azraq al-Fāreqī (d. 577 Lunar) who stated therein: "The aforementioned Hojjaᵗ was born on the 9th day of Rabi' ol-Awwal in the year 255 [Lunar], and it is [also] said that his date of birth is the eighth day of Sha'bān of the year 256 [Lunar], and this second [date] is more correct."[40]

It must be said that the correct opinion is actually the one that Eben Khalkān mentioned first concerning the birth of the Imām, i.e. that he was born on the Friday of the middle of the month of Sha'bān in the year 255, upon which date there is consensus among all of the Shī'a. Sound (sahīh) hadīth reports have reached us concerning this matter, and the great scholars among the ancients have emphasized the correctness of this date.

---

[39] Eben Athīr al-Jazrī, Ezzeddīn, al-Kāmel fī't-Tārīkh, 7:274 (at the end of the events of the year 260 Lunar).
[40] Eben Khalkān, Wafāt ol-A'yān, 4:176 and 4:562.

- Shaykh Koleynī, who lived through almost the entire period of the Lesser Occultation, has considered this date to be a given fact, giving preference to the veracity of hadīth reports that report this date in preference to other reports. He states: "Imām Mahdī ﷻ was born in the middle of the month of Sha'bān in the year 255."[41]

- Shaykh Saddūq (d. 381 Lunar) relates from his master, Mohammad b. Mohammad b. 'Asām al-Koleyni, who relates from Theqat ol-Islam Shaykh Mohammad b. Ya'qūb al-Koleynī, who has related a report from Ali b. Mohammad b. Bandār that "The Lord of the Age [the Imām al-Mahdī ﷻ] was born in the middle of the month of Sha'bān in the year 255."[42]

It is necessary to mention that Shaykh Koleynī has not attributed his report as having been related by Ali b. Mohammad b. Bandār because this report is widely recognized (mashhūr) and is acceptable to all.

3. Shamsoddīn adh-Dhahabī (d. 748 Lunar).
Shamsoddīn adh-Dhahabī avows to the birth of Imām Mahdī ﷻ in at least three of his books; (we have not investigated his other books). In his al-Ebar, he writes, "In the year 256 Lunar, Mohammad b. Hasan al-Askari ﷺ b. Alī al-Hādī ﷺ b.

---

[41] Koleynī, Shaykh, Shaykh Mohammad b. Ya'qūb, Theqat ol-Islam, Osūl al-Kāfī, 1:514 (Ch. 125).
[42] Saddūq, Shaykh, Kamāl od-Dīn, 2:430, Ch. 42.

Mohammad al-Jawād ﷺ b. Ali ar-Reḍā ﷺ b. Mūsā al-Kāẓem ﷺ b. Ja'far as-Ṣādeq ﷺ al-Alawī al-Hosaynī was born. He is the same Abol-Qāsem which the *rawāfeḍ*[43] call the *Hojja'*, and his honorifics are al-Mahdī (the Guided One), *al-Montaẓer* (the Awaited One) and *Ṣāheb oz-Zamān* (the Lord of the Age); and he is the last in the line of the Twelve Imāms."[44]

Dhahabī also writes in his *Tārīkh al-Islām* describing Imām Ḥasan Askarī ﷺ, "Ḥasan b. Ali b. Mohammad b. Ali ar-Reḍā b. Mūsā b. Ja'far as-Ṣādeq, Abū-Mohammad al-Hāshemī al-Hosaynī, is one of the Imāms of the Shī'a who believe in their immaculacy (esmaᵗ = sinlessness as well as inerrancy) and who is called Ḥasan Askarī ﷺ because he lived in Sāmarrā which used to be called Askar. He is the father of the Awaited Imām of the Rawāfeḍ who died on the 8th of Rabī' ol-Awwal in the year 260 at the age of 29 and was buried next to his father. But his son, Mohammad b. Ḥasan, who the Rawāfeḍ consider to be the One who will Arise [in insurrection to establish justice] (al-Qāem) and the Proof [of God] (al-Hojjaᵗ) was born in the year 258."[45]

---

[43] A derogatory term some Sunni use to refer to the Shī'a. Some employ the word *rāfeḍī* (plural, *rawāfeḍ*; refuser(s), rejector(s)) in order to demean and denigrate the Shī'a and as a technique to continue their conflation with extremist Gholāt views and with the views of other deviant sects, all of which they put in one basket and refer to as *rāfeḍī* and *rawāfeḍ*.

[44] Dhahabī, *al-Ebar fī Khabar man Ghabar*, 3:31.

[45] Dhahabī, Tārīkh al-Islam, 19:113 (under the events of the years 251 to 260).

Additionally, Dhahabī writes in Seyr E'lām ol-Anbīyā: "The Noble Awaited One, Abol-Qāsem Mohammad b. Hasan al-Askarī ﷺ b. Ali al-Hādī ﷺ b. Mohammad al-Jawād ﷺ b. Ali ar-Redā ﷺ b. Mūsā al-Kāzem ﷺ b. Ja'far as-Sādeq ﷺ b. Mohammad al-Bāqer ﷺ b. Zeyn ol-Ābedīn ﷺ b. al-Hosayn ash-Shahīd ﷺ b. al-Imām Alī b. Abī-Tāleb ﷺ al-Alawī al-Hosaynī ﷻ, is the last Imām of the series of Twelve Imāms."[46]

We have mentioned what we had in mind concerning the birth of Imām Mahdī ﷻ, but consider it necessary to say that, that which Dhahabī was awaiting was nothing but a mirage.

4. Eben al-Wardī (d. 749 Lunar).
In a concise supplement that has come to be known as the History of Eben al-Wardī we see the following: "Mohammad b. Hasan al-Khāles was born in the year 255."[47]

5. Ahmad Eben-Hajar al-Heythamī ash-Shāfeī (d. 974 Lunar).
In the last chapter of section eleven of as-Sawāeq ol-Mahraqa, Heythamī writes, "Abū-Mohammad al-Hasan al-Khāles who has been called al-Askarī by Eben Khalkān, was born in the year 232... and died at the age of 28, and was buried next to his father and maternal aunt. It is said that he was poisoned. He did not have any offspring other than Abol-Qāsem Mohammad al-Hojja', who was five years old at the time of his father's death,

---

[46] Dhahabī, Seyr E'lām ol-Anbīyā, 13:119, #60.
[47] Quoted in Nūr ol-Absār, page 186.

but whom God ﷻ bestowed wisdom upon at this age. He is referred to as the One who will Arise [in insurrection for justice] (al-Qāem) and the Awaited One (al-Montazer) because it is said that he disappeared from view in Medina and it is not known where he is."[48]

6. Shabrāwī ash-Shāfe'ī (d. 1171 Lunar).
Shabrāwī affirms in his book al-Ethāf that Imām Mahdī ﷻ Mohammad b. Hasan al-Askarī ﷻ was born in the middle of the month of Sha'bān in the year 255.[49]

7. Mo'men b. Hasan Shabalanjī (d. 1308 Lunar).
In his book Nūr ol-Absār, Shabalanjī refers to the name of Imām Mahdī ﷻ and to his noble lineage, his honorific and titles, and says, "He is the last Imām of the Twelve Imāms of the Imāmīya (Twelver) [Shī'a]."[50]

8. Khayreddīn Zarkalī (d. 1396 Lunar).
Zarkalī writes in his al-A'lām concerning the Awaited Imām al-Mahdī, "Mohammad b. Hasan al-Askarī b. Ali al-Hādī Abol-Qāsem is the last of the Imāms of the Twelvers… He was born in Sāmarrā. His father died when he was five and it is said that he was born in the middle of the month of Sha'bān in the year

---

[48] Ahmad Eben-Hajar al-Heythamī, as-Sawāeq ol-Mahraqa, p. 207 (1st ed.), p. 124 (2nd ed.), and pgs. 313 – 314 (3rd ed.).
[49] Page 68.
[50] Shabalanjī, Nūr ol-Absār, p. 186.

255 and that he entered into the Lesser Occultation in the year 265."⁵¹

It should be noted that in accordance with the consensus of Shī'a scholarly opinion, the year 260 Lunar is the start of the Lesser Occultation, and it is possible that the date which appears in Zarkalī's al-A'lām is a printing error, because Zarkalī has written the date in numerical (rather than alphabetical) form, which is a form which is conducive to such errors. For more information, the interested reader can refer to the book al-Mahdī al-Montazer fi'l-Fekr al-Islāmī, printed by the Markaz ar-Resāla, pages 123 to 127.

2 The Name and Lineage of Imām Mahdī

Anyone who studies the sound hadīth reports that are found in the Sunni compilations concerning the name and lineage of Imām Mahdī will see that emphasis has been placed on the fact that the Imām's lineage goes back to the Apostle of God and that he is one of the ahl al-bayt (the Members of the Household]of the Prophet]) and the last in the line of the Twelve Immaculate Imāms who has the title al-Mahdī al-Montazer (the Guided One who is Awaited). All of this is in accord with the beliefs of the Twelver Shī'a. Here it will suffice our purposes to provide a few examples of such references and descriptions.

---

⁵¹ Zarkalī, al-A'lām, 6:80.

1. The Imām al-Mahdī ﷻ described as a Canaanite, a Qurayshite and a Hashemite.

It is related from Qatāda: "I asked Saī'd b. Mosayyeb, 'Is it true [what they say about] the Mahdī?' He said, 'Yes, it is true.' I said, 'What nation is he from?' He said, 'He is a Canaanite.' I asked, 'What tribe is he from?' He said, 'He is of the Quraysh.' I asked, 'What clan is he from?' He said, 'He is of the Banī-Hāshem.'"[52]

2. The Imām al-Mahdī ﷻ described as a son of 'Abdol-Mottaleb.

Eben Māja relates from Anas b. Mālek that "The Apostle ﷺ of God ﷺ said, 'We the sons of 'Abdol-Mottaleb, meaning myself, and Hamza and Ali and Ja'far and Hasan and Hosayn and al-Mahdī, are the sādāt[53] of Heaven'."[54]

3. The Imām al-Mahdī ﷻ described as a son of Abū-Tāleb.

It is related from Seyf b. Omayr: "I was with al-Mansūr the Abbāsid [caliph] when suddenly he told me, 'O Seyf b. Omayr! Know that of a certainty a herald from the Heavens will make a call in the name of a man who is of the offspring of Abū-Tāleb.' I said, 'Would that I were sacrificed for you, O Commander of

---

[52] Moqaddasī ash-Shāfe'ī, E'qd ad-Dorar, p. 42-44, section one; Hākem al-Haskānī an-Neyshāpurī, al-Mostadrak 'alā's-Sahīhayn, 4:533; Heythamī, Ahmad Eben-Hajar, Majma' oz-Zawāed, 7:115.

[53] Princes, lords (especially applied to the descendants of Mohammad).

[54] Eben Māja, Sonan, 2:1368, Hadith#4087; Hākem al-Haskānī an-Neyshāpurī, al-Mostadrak 'alā's-Sahīhayn, 3:211; Soyūtī, Jalāloddīn, Jam' oj-Jawāme', 1:851.

the Faithful! Is this a hadīth that you are reporting?' He said, 'Yes, I swear [upon my oath] with He in Whose hands [the fate of] my soul rests that I heard this [report directly] with my [own] ears.' I said, I had not heard this report until now, O Commander of the Faithful!' He said, 'O Seyf! This call is the truth, and when it comes, we shall be the first people to respond to it. But this will be a calling to one of our paternal cousins.' I said, 'A man from the progeny of [Lady] Fātema ؟' He said, 'Yes, O Seyf! If it had not been for the fact that I have heard this hadīth report from Abū-Ja'far Mohammad b. Ali (Imām Bāqer) and that everyone relates it, I would not have accepted it [as being true], but I [did indeed] hear it from Mohammad b. Ali.'"[55]

4. The Imām al-Mahdī described as being one of the ahl al-bayt (the Members of the Household of the Prophet).

It is related from Abū-Sa'īd al-Khedrī that "the Apostle of God said, 'The Day of Resurrection will not arrive until there comes a time when the world will be filled with tyranny and injustice; at that time, a man from my lineage will appear who will fill the world with justice and equity when it had been filled with tyranny and injustice."[56]

---

[55] Moqaddasī ash-Shāfe'ī, E'qd ad-Dorar, Section 4, p.149-150.
[56] Ahmad, Masnad, 3:424, Hadith#10920; Abī-Ya'lā, Masnad, 2:274, Hadith#987; Mostadrak, 4:577; Aqd od-dorrar, 36, Chapter one; Mawārd oz-Zamān, 464, Hadith#1880 & 1879; Eben Khaldūn, Moqaddame, p.250 (Chapter 53); Soyūtī, Jalāloddīn, Jāme oj-Javame', 1:902. Mottaqī al-Hendī, Kanz ol-A'mmāl, 14:271, Hadith#8691. Qondūzī, Yanabī al-Mawadda, p. 433.

A report similar to this one has been related by Abdollāh b. Omar from the Apostle ﷺ of God, who said, "The Day of Resurrection will not arrive until a man from my Household (ahl baytī) appears who has the same name as me."⁵⁷ And it is reported by Ali ؏ that the Apostle ﷺ of God ﷻ said, "The Guided One (al-Mahdī) is from us, the Members of the Household [of the Prophet ﷺ], whose work God ﷻ will make whole."⁵⁸

---

⁵⁷ Masnad ol-Bazzāz, 1:281; Ahmad, Masnad, p. 3761; Sonan ot-Termezī, 55:4, Chapter 52, Hadith#2230; Al-Mo'jam ol-Kabir, 10:135, Hadith#10221; Tarīkh ol-Baghdād, 4:388; Aqd od-Dorrar, p. 38 (Chapter 3); Matāleb os-So'ūl, 2:81; Mohammad Nūfeylī Qurayshī Ganjī Shafe'ī, al-Bayan fī Akhbār-e Saheb oz-Zamān, p 91; Farā'ed os-Samtayn, 2:327, Hadith#576; Soyūtī, Ad-Dorr ol-Manthur, 6:58; Jam' oj-Jawāme', 1:903; Kanz ol-Ammāl, 14:271, Hadith#38962; Borhān ol-Mottaqī, p. 90 (Chapter 2), Hadith#4.

³¹ Ketāb-e Eben Abī-Shayba, 678:8, Hadith#190; Ebne Hammād, Fatan; Ahmad, Masnad, 1:84; at-Tarīkh Bokhārī, 1:371, Hadith#994; Eben Māja, Sonan, 2:136, Chapter 34, Hadith#4085; Abī-Ya'lā, Masnad, 1:359, Hadith#465; Helīyaᵗ ol-Owlīā, 3:177; Eben Odā, al-Kāmel, 7:2643; al-Ferdows, 4:222, Hadith#6619; Ganjī Shafe'ī, al-Bayan fī Akhbār-e Saheb oz-Zamān, p.100; Aqd od-Dorrar, p. 183 (Chapter 6); Soyutī, Al-Elal ol-Hāwī, 2:213; Soyutī, Dorr ol-Manthur, 6:58; Jam' ol-Javame', 1:449; Al-Jāme' ol-Saghīr, 2:672, Hadith#9243; Eben Hajar, as-Sawā'eq, p.163 (Chapter 511), Chapter 1; Mottaqī al-Hendī, Kanz ol-A'mmāl, 14:264, Hadith#38664; Borhān ol-Mottaqī, p.87 (Chapter 1), Hadith#43; Merqāt ol-Mafātīh, 9:349; Feyz ol-Qadīr, 6:278, Hadith#9243.

5. The Imām al-Mahdī ﷻ described as being one of the progenies of the Prophet ﷺ of God ﷻ.

A report has been related by Abdollāh b. Omar from the Apostle ﷺ of God, who said, "At the end of time (ākhar oz-zamān) a man will appear who is one of my progenies, who has the same name as me, and who has the same honorific (konya) as me. He will fill the world with equity and justice after it will have become filled with tyranny and injustice. He is the Guided One (al-Mahdī)."[59]

6. The Imām al-Mahdī ﷻ described as being one of the progenies of Lady Fātema ﷻ.

It is related from Omm Salāma (may God ﷻ be pleased with her), one of the wives of the Prophet ﷺ, that he said, "[The coming of] the Mahdī is real and he will be one of the progenies of Lady Fātema ﷻ."[60] Omm Salāma (may God ﷻ be pleased with her) has also related, "I heard the Prophet ﷺ of God ﷻ say, "The Mahdī is of my family (*etratī*) and is of the progeny of Lady Fātema ﷻ."[61]

---

[59] Eben Jowzī, Tazkerat ol-Khawās, p. 33; Aqd od-Dorrar, p. 43 (Chapter 1); Eben Taymīya, Menhāj as-Sonnat an-Nabawīya, 4:86-87.

[60] Tarīkh ot-Tabarī, 3:364; Tabarānī, al-Ma'jam ol-Kabīr, 23:267, Hadith#566; Hākem al-Haskānī an-Neyshāpūrī, al-Mostadrak fī Sahīhayn, 4:557.

[61] Abu-Dāwud, as-Sonan, 4:104, Hadith#4284; Eben Māja, as-Sonan, 2:1368, Chapter 34, Hadith#4086; al-Ferdows, 4:497, Hadith#6943; Masābīh ol-Boghawī, 3:492, Chapter 3, Hadith#4211; Jāme' ol-Osul,

7. The Imām al-Mahdī ﷻ described as being one of the progenies of Imām Hosayn ؏.

It is related from Hodhayfaᵗ b. Yammān that "One day the Apostle ﷺ of God ﷻ delivered a sermon to us in which he stated, '[Even] if [it be the case that] only a single day remains [of the life] of the world, God ﷻ will lengthen it until a man from my progeny who has the same name as me appears.' Salman the Persian asked, 'From which of your children [will he be from]. O Apostle ﷺ of God?' The Prophet ﷺ said, 'From this child of mine.' And he patted al-Hosayn ؏ on the back."⁶²

It is reported from Abū-Saī'd al-Kedrī that "The Apostle ﷺ of God ﷻ fell ill one day, from which [illness] he recovered. While he was ill, his daughter [Lady] Fātema ؏ came to visit him while I was seated to the right of the Apostle ﷺ of God ﷻ. When

---

5:343; Matāleb ol-So'ul, p. 8; Aqd od-Dorrar, p. 36 (Chapter 1); Mīzān ol-E'tedāl, 2:87; Meshkāᵗ ol-Masābīh, 3:24, Chapter 2, Hadith#5453; Tohfaᵗ ol-Ashrāf, 13:7, Hadith#18153; aj-Jāme ol-Saghīr, 2:672, Hadith#9241; Soyutī, Dorr ol-Manthūr, 6:58; Soyutī, Jam oj-Javāme',1:449; Eben Hajar, as-Sawā'eq ol-Mahraqa, p.141 (Chapter 11); Mottaqī al-Hendī, Kanz ol-A'mmāl, 14:262, Hadith#38662; Merqāt ol-Mafātīh, 9:350; As'āf or-Rāghebīn, p.145; Feyz ol-Ghadīr, 6:277, 9241; at-Tāj oj-Jāme ol-Osul, 5:343.

⁶² Eben Qayyem, al-Menār ol-Monīf, p. 329 & 148, Chapter 50, quoted in Tabarānī's al-Osāt; Aqd od-Dorrar, p. 45 (Chapter 1); Moheb-e Tabarī, Zakhā'er ol-Oqbā, p. 136; Hamawānī, Farāed as-Samtayn, 2:275 & 325.

[Lady] Fātema ﷺ saw her father's weakness and state of ill health, she was overcome with emotion and tears welled up in her eyes and ran down her face. The Apostle ﷺ of God ﷻ asked her, 'Why are you crying, O Fātema ﷺ?' Do you not know that Almighty God ﷻ looked down on Earth and chose your father from among its inhabitants as His Apostle? And then He looked down on Earth again and chose your husband and revealed to me [the command] to select him for your husband and to make him my wasī (inheritor, legatee, executor, and successor)? Do you not know that you have been subject to the grace and generosity of God ﷻ whereby your father has favored you by [wedding you to] the most learned person, the one with the greatest forbearance [of character], and the first man to enter into Islam?'

"[Lady] Fātema ﷺ became contented and smiled. The Apostle ﷺ of God ﷻ wanted to point out more of the favors which God ﷻ had bestowed on Mohammad ﷺ and his Family ﷺ; he therefore said,

'O Fātema ﷺ! Ali ﷺ has eight special virtues: faith in God ﷻ and his Apostle ﷺ, wisdom, being your husband, being the father of al-Hasan ﷺ and al-Hosayn ﷺ, and being [the living embodiment of the principle of] enjoining the doing of that which is right and forbidding the doing of that which is wrong. O Fātema ﷺ! Six virtues have been given to us, the Members of the Household [of the Prophet ﷺ] which have not been given to anyone else and which none other than us, the Members of the

Household [of the Prophet ﷺ], can realize. Our prophet is the best of the prophets, and that is your father; our *wasi* (inheritor, legatee, executor, and successor) is the best of the *owsiā* (the plural of wasī), and that is your husband; our martyr is the best of the martyrs, and that is your uncle Hamza; the grandchildren of this community (omma') belong to us, and these are your children al-Hasan ؏ and al-Hosayn ؏; and the Mahdī of this community (omma') belongs to us, behind whom Jesus ؏ will pray.' The Prophet ﷺ then placed his hand on the shoulder of al-Hosayn ؏ and said, 'The Mahdī of this community will be one of the children [from the progeny] of this Imām.'"[63]

8. The Imām al-Mahdī ؏ and his mother described as being of the progeny of Imām as-Sādeq ؏.
The renowned exegete of the Qoran Abdollāh b. Ahmad Eben Khashshāb has related, "Abol-Qāsem Tāher b. Mūsā al-Kāzem reports from his father and his grandfather that Ja'far b. Mohammad ؏ said, 'The righteous posterity (al-khalaf as-sāleh) is one of my progenies, who will be the Mahdī of this community. His name is Mohammad and his honorific is Abol-Qāsem, and he will appear at the end of time. His mother's name is Narjes and there will always be a cloud over him to protect him from [the harsh rays of] the sun. This cloud always moves with him

---

[63] al-Bayān, p. 120 (Chapter 9); Eben Sabbāq al-Mālekī, al-Fosūl al-Mohemma, p. 286, Published by Dār ol-Azvā', Chapter 12; Qondūzī, Yanabī al-Mawadda, p. 493 & 490, Chapter 94.

and will announce with a distinct voice that this is the Mahdī and that you should follow [and obey] him.'"⁶⁴

9. The Imām al-Mahdī ﷻ described as being one of the progenies of Imām ar-Redā ؑ.

It has been reported from Hasan b. al-Khāled: "Ali b. Mūsā ar-Redā ؑ said, 'One who does not have devoutness and piety does not have religion, and the most valued person in the sight of God ﷻ is the one with the greatest amount of piety.' Imām Redā ؑ then said, 'The mother of the offspring of the fourth [generation] of my progeny is the best of bondsmaidens. God ﷻ will render the world free of any and all tyranny and injustice by means of her son.'"⁶⁵

10. The name of the father of the Imām al-Mahdī ﷻ.

Rowyānī, Tabarānī and others have reported: the Mahdī is one of the progenies of the Apostle ﷺ of God ﷻ whose face shines like a star. His facial features are that of an Arab and his stature is that of an Israelite (= tall). He will fill the world with justice and equity whereas it was filled with injustice and tyranny [hitherto]. The creatures of the world and of the heavens will be content with his reign. It is also said of him that he is young, has

---

⁶⁴ Qondūzī, *Yanabī al-Mawadda*, p.491, quoting from Hāfez Abuna'īm Esfahānī, Arba'īn.
⁶⁵ Qondūzī, *Yanabī al-Mawadda*, p. 489 & 448, from the book *Farā'ed os-Samtayn*.

brown eyes, thick eyebrows, a straight nose, a full beard, and has a freckle on his right cheek.

Mohīyeddīn Eben Arabī has said in The Meccan Openings, "Know that of a certainty the Mahdī will appear, but his rise will not be effected until a time when the world has become full of iniquity and injustice, and he shall render it full of justice and equity. He is of the Family of the Apostle of God and is of the progeny of [Lady] Fātema. Hosayn b. Alī b. Abī-Tāleb is his ancestor and his father is Imām Hasan al-Askarī. He has the same name as the Apostle of God and the Muslims will pledge allegiance to him between the Rokn (Station) [of the Black Stone] and the Maqām (Station) [of Abraham].[66] He is similar to the Apostle of God in his outward appearance and in his character and behavior, and the Kūfans will be the ones who benefit most from his [advent]. He will distribute the wealth [of the community] justly, and His Eminence Khedr will be at his side."[67]

---

[66] Two stations or fixed places of religious significance at the Ka'ba or the Sacred Sanctuary, the House of God in Mecca.

[67] Sheykh Hasan Addowī Hamzāwī Mesrī, Mashāreq ol-Anwār fī fūz Ahl ol-E'tebār, p. 476-477; Faslū fī Mahdī, Yawāqīt oj-Jawāher, p. 562; Bāb Ashrāt os-Sā't, quoting from Fotūhāt ol-Makkīya, Chapter 366.

3 The Characteristics of Imām Mahdī

Having surveyed the hadīth reports relating to the names and lineage of the Imām al-Mahdī ﷻ, we shall now proceed to an examination of the hadīth reports relating to his attributes which appear in the Sunni compilations of hadīth.

1. Abū-Sa'īd al-Khedrī has related from the Apostle ﷺ of God: "The Mahdī is of me; he has a luminous forehead and a straight nose. He shall fill the world with justice and equity after it has become full of iniquity and injustice."[68]

2. Khodhayfa has related from the Apostle ﷺ of God: "The Mahdī is one of my progenies whose face shines as brightly as a full moon. His facial features are that of an Arab and his stature is that of an Israelite (= tall). He shall fill the world with justice and equity after it has become full of iniquity and injustice. The

---

[68] Abu-Dāwud, as-Sonan, 4:107, Hadith#428; Hākem al-Haskānī an-Neyshāpurī, al-Mostadrak 'Alā's-Sahīhayn, 4:557 (with a slight variation); Ma'ālem os-Sonan, 4:344; Masābīh ol-Nabghawī, 3:492, Hadith#4212, al-Elal ol-Motenāhyaᵗ, 2:859, Hadith#1443; Jāme' ol-Osul, 5:343, Chapter 7, Matāleb ol-Osul, 2:80, Hadith#12; Al-Bayān, p. 117; Aghd od-Dorrar, p. 59 (Chapter 3); Meshkāᵗ ol-Masābīh, 3:171 (Chapter 2), Chapter 2 Hadith#5454; Al-Jāme' os-Saghīr, 2:672, Hadith#9244; Jam' ol-Javāme', 1:449; Mottaqī al-Hendī, Kanz ol-A'mmāl, 14:264, Hadith#38665; Merqat ol-Mafātīh, 9:351, Hadith#5454; Feyz ol-qadīr, 6:278, Hadith#9244; AL-Tāj ol-Javāme' lel-osul, 5:343, Chapter 7.

creatures of the world and of the heavens and even the birds of the skies will be contented with his reign."⁶⁹

3. Abū-Sa'īd al-Khedrī has related from the Apostle ﷺ of God: "The Mahdī is from us, the Members of the Household [of the Prophet ﷺ]; he has a tall and upright stature and a luminous forehead. He shall fill the world with justice and equity after it has become full of iniquity and injustice."⁷⁰

4. Qatāda relates from Abdollāh b. Harth: "The Mahdī will make his appearance as a man of forty years of age, and he will appear like an Israelite [in his outward features]."⁷¹

---

⁶⁹ al-Ferdows, 4:496, Hadith#6940; Al-Elal ol-Motenāhyaᵗ, 2:858, Hadith#1439; Al-Bayān, p. 118 (Chapter 8); Zakhā'er ol-Oqbā, p. 136; Aqd od-Dorrar, p. 60 (Chapter 3); Mīzān Ol-E'tedāl, 3:449; Al-Bayān ol-Mīzān, 5:24; Eben Sabbāq al-Mālekī, al-Fosūl al-Mohemma, p. 284; Al-Jāme' ol-Saghīr, 2:672, Hadith#9245; Eben Hajar, as-Sawā'eq ol-Mahraqa, p. 164 (Chapter 11) Chapter 1; Mottaqī al-Hendī, Kanz ol-A'mmāl, 14:264, Hadith#38666; Merqat ol-Mafāt, 9:350; Lawā'eh os-Safāvīnī, 2:4; As'āf or-Rāghebīn, p.146; Nur ol-Absār, p. 187; Feyz ol-Ghadīr, 6:279, Hadith#9245;

⁷⁰ Hākem al-Haskānī an-Neyshāpurī, al-Mostadrak 'Alā's-Sahīhayn, 4:557; Aqd od-dorrar, p.60 (Chapter 3); farā'ed os-Samtīn, 2:330, Hadith#580, Borhān ol-Mottaqī, p. 98 (Chapter 2), Hadith#28 & p.99 (Chapter 3) Hadith#3; Qondūzī, Yanabī al-Mawadda, p. 448 (Chapter 94).

⁷¹ Fatan Eben Hammād, p. 258, Hadith#1008; Al-Hāwī, 2:232; Borhān ol-Mottaqī, p.99 (Chapter 3), Hadith#2; Mottaqī al-Hendī, Kanz ol-A'mmāl, 14:586, Hadith#39660.

5. It is related by Mohammad b. Jobayr: "The Mahdī has thick eyebrows that are separated from each other, and has dark eyes. His advent will be from the Hejāz[72] and he will [go from there to] become established on the pulpit [of the congregational mosque] of Damascus. He will be eighteen years of age when this occurs."[73]

6. It is related from Abdollāh b. Bashīr from Ka'b: "The humility and submissiveness of the Mahdī towards God is such that it is like an eagle who has spread his wings [and placed them] over the earth."[74]

7. It is related by Eben Abbās: "The Mahdī is a youth who is from us, the Members of the Household [of the Prophet]."[75]

---

[72] The western sector of Arabia that borders the Red Sea and where Mecca and Medina are located.

[73] Borhān ol-Mottaqī, p. 100 (Chapter 3), Hadith#3; Aqd od-Dorrar, p. 63-64 (Chapter 3); Alhāwi, 2:232; Farā'ed Fawā'ed ol-Fekr, p. 4 (Chapter 2)

[74] Fatan Eben Hammād, p. 258; Aqd od-Dorrar, p. 65 (Chapter 3); Al-Hāwī, 2:232; Al-qol el-Mokhtasar, p. 98 (Chapter 3), Hadith#29; ; Borhān ol-Mottaqī, p. 101 (Chapter 3), Hadith#29; ; Borhān ol-Mottaqī, p. 101 (Chapter 3), Hadith#10.

[75] Fatn Eben Hammād, p. 102; Al-Hāwī, 2:232; Borhān ol-Mottaqī, p. 98 (Chapter 2), Hadith#27 & 21; Mottaqī al-Hendī, Kanz ol-A'mmāl, Hadith#39658 (with a little difference); Farā'ed Fawā'ed ol-Fekr, p. 2 (Chapter 10).

8. Abdor-Rahmān b. 'Owf relates from his father that the Apostle of God stated, "God will commission a man from my Family whose front teeth have gaps and whose forehead is luminous. He shall fill the world with justice and equity after it has become full of iniquity and injustice, and will give generously of his wealth."[76]

9. Mohammad b. Ja'far relates from Alī b. Abī-Tāleb: "This son of mine, al-Hosayn, is a prince and a lord; just as the Apostle of God has named him seyyed (prince, lord). Soon Almighty God will create a person from his seed who has the same name as your prophet, and is similar to him in his outward appearance as well as in his character and personality. He will make his appearance in conditions wherein the people live in neglect [of their duties to God and to their Imām], and have despoiled his right and have [thereby] made injustice and inequity prevail. ... The creatures in the heavens will be pleased with his insurrection [against the forces of tyranny]. He has a luminous forehead, a straight nose, a raised chest and smooth cheeks, and a black freckle can be seen on his right cheek. Gaps

---

[76] Al-Bayān, p. 139 (Chapter 19); Aqd od-Dorrar, p. 37 (Chapter 1); Farā'ed ol-Mosattīn, 2:231, Hadith#582; Al-Hāwī, 2:220; Eben Hajar, As-Sawā'eq ol-Moharreqa, p. 164 (Chapter 11), Chapter 2; AL-qol el-Mokhtasar, p. 43 (Chapter 1), Hadith#33; Borhān ol-Mottaqī, p.84 (Chapter 1), Hadith#32; As'āf or-rāghebīn, p. 146; Qondūzī, Yanabī al-Mawadda, p. 436 & 433 (Chapter 73), Chapter 2; Farā'ed Fawā'ed ol-Fekr, p. 4 (Chapter 2).

can be seen in his front teeth, and he shall fill the world with justice and equity after it has become full of iniquity and injustice."[77]

10. It is related from Solaymān b. Habīb: "I heard from Abū-Amāma al-Bāhalī that the Apostle of God said, 'Peace will reign between you and Rūm (Byzantium) for four periods; the fourth peace will be broken by a man from the family of Heraclius, and this [period] will span seven years.' Someone asked, 'O Apostle of God! Who will be in charge of the people at that time?' The Prophet said, 'My progeny, the Mahdī, who will be forty years of age [at the time]. His face will shine like a star, and a black freckle will be seen on his right cheek."[78]

11. Haytham b. Abdor-Rahmān relates from Alī b. Abī-Tāleb: "The Mahdī will be born in Medina. He is of the Household of the Prophet and has the same name as him. He shall

---

[77] Abu-Dāwud, as-Sonan, 4:108, Hadith#429; Jāme' ol-Osūl, 5:343; Abī Dāwud, al-Mokhtasar, 6:162, Hadith#4121; Aqd od-Dorrar, p. 45 (Chapter 1); Fatan Eben Kathīr, 1:38; Eben Khaldun, Moqaddama, p. 391, Chapter 53; Al-Hāwī, 2:214; Soyutī, Dorr ol-Manthūr, 6:39, under the āya 18; Jam' oj-Jawāme', 2:35; Mottaqī al-Hendī, Kanz ol-A'mmāl, 16:647, Hadith#27636; Merqāt ol-Mafātīh, 9:363, Hadith#5462; Qondūzī, Yanabī al-Mawadda, p. 432 (Chapter 72); At-Tāj oj-Jawāme' Lel-Osul, 5:343, Hadith#10.
[78] Al-Bayān, p. 137-138 (Chapter 18), quoting from al-Mo'jam ol-Kabīr & Abu No'aym's Manāqeb ol-Mahdī.

migrate to Jerusalem. He will have a full beard and black eyes and bright teeth. A black freckle will be seen on his [right] cheek. His banner will be square and will be made of black velvet. God 🕌 will aid him by way of three thousand angels, who will strike at the faces and backs of his adversaries."[79]

4 The Rank of Imām Mahdī before God

In this section, we will point to Imām Mahdī's rank and station before God 🕌.

1. It is related by Anas b. Mālek that the Apostle 🕌 of God 🕌 said, "We the children of Abdol-Mottaleb; that is, me, Hamza, Ali, Ja'far, Hasan, Hosayn and Mahdī, are the Masters of Heaven."[80]

---

[79] Al-Bayān, p.140, quoting from Al-Mo'jam Tabarānī & Abu No'aym's Manāqeb ol-Mahdī.

[80] Eben Māja, Sonan, 2:1368, Chapter 34, Hadith#4087; Hākem al-Haskānī an-Neyshāpurī, al-Mostadrak 'Alā's-Sahīhayn, 3:211; Khatīb al-Baghdādī, Tarīkh al-Baghdād, Hadith#5050; Matāleb os-So'ūl, 2:81; al-Bayān, p. 101 (Chapter 3); Tabarī, Mohebbeddīn, Dhakhāer ol-Oqbā, pgs. 15 & 89; Tabarī, Mohebbeddīn, ar-Rīyāḍ an-Naḍra, 3:4 & 3:182; 'Aqd od-Dorrar, p. 194; Farā'ed os-Samtayn, 2:32, Hadith#370; Moqaddama, p. 398, Chapter 53; Eben Hajar, as-Sawā'eq ol-Mahraqa,p.160 ; Soyūtī, Jam' oj-Jawāme', 1:851;Eben Hajar, as-Sawā'eq ol-Mahraqa,p.160& p.187; Borhān ol-Mottaqī, p. 89, Hadith#3; As'āf or-rāghebīn, p. 124; Alhāvī 2:214.

His Eminence, the Imām al-Mahdī

2. It is related by Eben Abbās that the Apostle ﷺ of God ﷻ said, "Mahdī is the Peacock of the denizens of Heaven."[81]

3. It is related by Abū-Horayra that the Apostle ﷺ of God ﷻ said, "A caliph will appear in this community over whom neither Abū-Bakr nor Omar have preeminence."[82]

4. It is related by Abdollāh b. Omar that the Apostle ﷺ of God ﷻ said, "The Mahdī will appear while there is a cloud over his head, and this cloud will issue forth a call, saying, 'This is the caliph of God, the Mahdī; follow [and obey] him.'"[83]

5. It is also related by Abdollāh b. Omar that the Apostle ﷺ of God ﷻ said, "The Mahdī will appear while there is an angel over his head, and this angel will issue forth a call, saying, 'This is the caliph of God, the Mahdī; follow [and obey] him.'"[84]

---

[81] 7:2643; Al-Ferdows 4:222, Hadith #6668; al-Bayan p.118; Aqd od-Dorrar, p. 199; al-Fosūl al-Mohemma p. 248; Borhān ol-Mottaqī, p. 171; Hadith#2; Konūz od-Daqāeq p. 152; Nur ol-Absār, p. 187&p. 189; Yanabī al-Mawadda p. 181.

[82] Abī-Shayba, al-Masnaf 15:198, Hadith#19496; Eben Odayy Alkāmel 6:2433; ; Aqd od-dorrar, p.199; Borhān ol-Mottaqī Hadith#6.

[83] Albayān p.132; Aqd od-dorrar, p.183; Farā'ed os-Samtayn 2:316, Hadith#566&569; al-Fosūl al-Mohemma p.289; Alhāvī 2:217; Tārīkh ol-Khamīs 2:288; Nur ol-Absār, pgs. 188&189.

[84] Talkhīs ol-Motashābeha 1:417; Albayān p.133 ; Farā'ed os-Samtayn 2:316, Hadith #569; Alhāvī 2:217; Al-qol el-Mokhtasar, p. 39,

5 Imām Mahdī as the Caliph of God ﷻ and the Final Imām

In this chapter we examine the question as to whether another Imām will appear after the Mahdī, or whether he will be the final Imām, as is the belief of the Shī'a who await his advent?

1. It is related by Thowbān that the Apostle ﷺ of God ﷻ said, "'Three people will fight with you, all of whom are sons of caliphs, but none will be successful. Black flags will come from the east, and an intense battle will ensue' ... Here the Apostle ﷺ of God ﷻ said something which I do not recall, and then he said, 'When you see him, make haste in pledging your allegiance to him, even if [you have to do so] on your hands and knees, and on snow. Verily, he is the Mahdī, the caliph of God ﷻ."[85]

2. It is reported by Alī b. Abī-Tāleb ؏ who said, "I asked the Apostle ﷺ of God ﷻ if the Mahdī is of us, the Members of the Household [of the Prophet ﷺ], or is other than of us? He said, 'He is of us. Religion will end with us, just as it began with us.

Hadith#24; Borhān ol-Mottaqī, p.72, Hadith#2; Yanabī al-Mawadda, p. 447.

[85] al-Ganjī ash-Shāfe'ī, Mohammad b. Yūsof b. Mohammad, al-Bayān fī Akhbār Sāheb oz-Zamān, p. 104 (Chapter 3); Eben Māja, Sonan, 2:1367, Hadith#4084; Hākem al-Haskānī an-Neyshāpurī, al-Mostadrak 'Alā's-Sahīhayn, 4:463; Dhahabī, Talkhīs al-Mostadrak 'Alā's-Sahīhayn, 4:463-64; Ahmad b. Hanbal, Masnad, 5:277 (with a slight variation).

The people will be saved from misguidance and error by means of [someone from] us, just as they were saved from the error of idolatry by us. God ﷻ places affection for religion in the hearts of men by means of us, after they had become afflicted with enmity [toward each other] due to intrigues and sedition, just as God ﷻ created affection and friendship between them after there had been the enmity that resulted from their idolatry'."[86]

3. Eben Hajar al-Haythamī (d. 974 Lunar) writes: "Abū-Hosayn al-Ābrī said, 'The hadīth reports from the Prophet ﷺ concerning the Mahdī and his advent have reached the threshold of *tawātor*,[87] and numerous narrators have reported that the Mahdī will be a Member of the Household of the Prophet ﷺ, will fill the world with justice, and that Jesus ﷺ will pray behind him[88] [upon his Second Coming]."[89]

4. Shaykh Sabān (d. 1206 Lunar) has said, "Motewāter hadīth reports have been related from the Most Noble Prophet ﷺ which state that the Mahdī will appear and that he will be a

---

[86] Tabarī, al-Ma'jam ol-Owsat, 1:136, Hadith#157; al-Ganjī ash-Shāfe'ī, Mohammad b. Yūsof b. Mohammad, al-Bayān fī Akhbār Sāheb oz-Zamān, p. 125 (Chapter 11); Aqd od-dorrar, p. 192, Chapter 7; Heythamī, Majma' oz-Zawāed, 7:316-17; Eben Khaldūn, Moqaddame, p. 396-397 (Chapter 53); etc.

[87] See footnote #7 on page 39.

[88] This expression means that he will defer to him in prayer and to his superiority of spiritual rank.

[89] Eben Hajar, as-Sawā'eq ol-Mahraqa, p. 165.

Member of the Household of the Prophet ﷺ, that he will fill the world with peace and justice, and that Jesus ؏ will help him kill the Dajjāl (the anti-Christ) in Bāb ol-Lod[90] in the land of Palestine, and that he will lead the community and Jesus will pray behind him."[91]

5. Abū-Saī'd has reported that "The world will become filled with oppression and injustice and at that time, a man from the Family of the Prophet ﷺ will appear..."[92]

6 Jesus will Defer to the Mahdī

The hadīth reports which are available in the Sunni compilations provide us with the name and lineage of the Imām al-Mahdī as well as providing us with a description of his character and outward appearance. The question which now arises is whether there are any other signs during the era of his advent that would increase the people's confidence and faith in him and prevent them from being deceived by other false prophets? The hadīth reports stress the point that the prophet Jesus ؏ will return from the heavens and will defer to the Imām al-Mahdī.

---

[90] A village near Jerusalem.
[91] As'āf or-rāghebīn, p.140.
[92] Hākem al-Haskānī an-Neyshāpurī, al-Mostadrak 'Alā's-Sahīhayn, 4:558.

1. Eben Abī-Shayba relates from Eben Sīrīn in al-Mosannaf that "Imām Mahdī ﷻ is from this community and Jesus ﷺ will defer to him."[93]

2. Abū-Noaym has reported from Abdollāh b. Omar that "Jesus ﷺ the son of Mary ﷺ will come down from the heavens and will pray behind the Mahdī."[94]

3. Commenting on the hadīth report that says, "One of us behind whom Jesus ﷺ the son of Mary ﷺ will pray", Mīnāwī says, "[The person] referred to [in the report] is His Eminence the Imām al-Mahdī ﷻ behind whom [the prophet] Jesus ﷺ will pray after his descent from the heavens at the time of the appearance of the Dajjāl (the anti-Christ)."[95]

4. Eben Borhān, the Shāfe'ī scholar writes concerning the descent of Jesus ﷺ: "Jesus will descend [from heaven] at the time of the morning prayer and will pray behind the Imām al-Mahdī, and this will occur after the Mahdī says to him, 'Take the lead, O Rūhollāh[96] (O Spirit of God)!' But His Eminence Jesus ﷺ will say, 'You lead [the communal prayer service], as God ﷻ has appointed you [to this honor].'" Eben Borhān continues, "Jesus appears at the advent of the Mahdī and helps him kill the Dajjāl

---

[93] Abī-Shayba, al-Mosnaf, 15:198.
[94] Soyutī, al-Hāwī li'l-Fatāwā, 2:78.
[95] Mīnāwī, Fayḍ ol-Ghadīr, 6:17.
[96] The Quranic title for the great prophet Jesus ﷺ.

(the anti-Christ), and it is related in hadīth reports that the Mahdī is of the Family of the Most Noble Prophet ﷺ and is of the progeny of [Lady] Fātema ﷏."[97]

5. Eben Hajar al-Asqalānī writes in his Fath al-Bārī, "Abol-Hasan al-Khas'ī al-Ābdī[98] has stated in *Manāqeb al-Imām ash-Shāfe'ī* 'The hadīth reports [from the Prophet ﷺ] have reached the threshold of *tawātor*[99] that the Mahdī will be from this community and that Jesus ﷇ will defer to him in prayer.' He [Abol-Hasan al-Khas'ī al-Ābdī] has written this in refutation of a hadīth report which [Eben] Māja has related from [Mālek b.] Anas to the effect that there will be no Mahdī other than Jesus. [Eben Hajar's paraphrase of the report brought by al-Khas'ī al-Ābdī continues:] 'Subsequent [to Jesus's] advent, he [the Mahdī] asks Jesus ﷇ to lead [the communal prayer, and hence to lead the community], but Jesus declines [in his favor].'

Eben Hajar al-Asqalānī then states, "Jesus's deferral to a man from this community at the end of time and on the eve of the Resurrection is grounds for the veracity of the belief that the world will never be [left] without a hojjatollāh (God's proof [to humanity]), and God ﷻ is all-knowing."[100]

---

[97] Eben Borhān ash-Shāfe'ī, as-Sīrat al-Halabīa, 1:226-27.

[98] Ābrī is the correct orthography, and some have considered his patronymic to be Abol-Hosayn, whereas the correct version is Abol-Hasan. He died in 363 Lunar.

[99] See footnote #7 on page 39.

[100] Eben Hajr al-Asqalānī, Fath ol-Bārī, 6:383-85.

6. Eben Abī-Shayba reports from Eben Sīrīn that "The Mahdī is of this community and he shall be the person who will lead Jesus ﷺ, the son of Mary ﷺ [in the communal prayer service]."¹⁰¹

7 The Banner of Imām Mahdī

Among the signs of Imām Mahdī ﷻ that will increase the people's confidence and faith in him and prevent them from being deceived by others is his banner. The Imām's flag is like a sign that draws people toward him. Here we refer to two hadīth reports in this respect:

1. It is reported by Abdollāh b. Sharīk that "The banner of the Apostle ﷺ of God ﷻ is with the Mahdī. Would that I could be [there] in his presence [during his advent], for I would [surely] shout [for joy]!"¹⁰²

2. Eben Eshāq reports from Nowf al-Bakāī: "[The following slogan] is inscribed on the banner of Imām Mahdī ﷻ: al-bay'aᵗ li'lāh (Allegiance [only] to God)."¹⁰³

---

[101] Abī-Shayba, al-Mosnaf, 15:198, Hadith#19495.
[102] Eben Hāmed, Fatan, p. 249, Hadith#972; al-Qowl al-Mokhtasar, p. 100, Chapter 3, Hadith#35; Borhān ol-Mottaqī, p. 152 (Chapter 7), Hadith#24.
[103] Eben Hāmed, Fatan, p. 249, Hadith#973; Aqd od-Dorrar, p. 274 (Chapter 9); al-Qowl al-Mokhtasar, p. 101, Chapter 3, Hadith#36;

8 The Generosity and Largesse of Imām Mahdī

There is no doubt that in the reign of the Mahdī justice will prevail in all its dimensions and the earth and the skies will present the full measure of their bounty, and that his reign will be a universal one in which there is no oppression or injustice, and where mankind will attain to its felicity. We shall point to a few of the reports that provide the grounds for this belief.

1. Abū-Saī'd al-Khedrī related from the Most Noble Prophet: "During the time of the Mahdī, the community will be engulfed in the blessings and bounty [of God] the likes of which have not been seen. The skies will continually rain down on them, and there will not be a single plant that does not see its growth. And wealth is in such abundance that the request of anyone who asks the Mahdī for something will be granted."[104]

2. Abū-Saī'd al-Khedrī has also related from the Most Noble Prophet: "In my community, the Mahdī will appear, and he will reign for at least seven, or nine years. During his reign, the community will be so immersed in the blessings and bounty [of God], the likes of which they have not seen [hitherto]. At that

---

Borhān ol-Mottaqī, p. 152 (Chapter 7), Hadith#25; Farā'ed Fawā'ed ol-Fekr, p. 8 (Chapter 4); Qondūzī, Yanabī al-Mawadda, p. 435.

[104] Eben Hāmed, Fatan, p. 253, Hadith#992; Aqd od-Dorrar, p. 225 (Chapter 8); al-Ganjī ash-Shāfe'ī, Mohammad b. Yūsof b. Mohammad, al-Bayān fī Akhbār Sāheb oz-Zamān, p. 145 (Chapter 23); Eben Sabbāq al-Mālekī, al-Fosūl al-Mohemma, pgs. 288 – 289; Nūr ol-Absār, p. 189.

time, the earth will give of its bounty and will hold nothing back. During that time, wealth will be in such abundance that the request of anyone who asks the Mahdī for something will be granted."[105]

3. Abū-Saī'd al-Khedrī has related in yet another report from the Most Noble Prophet: "Verily, the Mahdī will appear in my community and will reign for five (or seven or nine) years – the doubt concerning the timing is the [original] narrator's. In those days, the request of anyone who asks the Mahdī for help will be granted to the extent of the petitioner's ability to carry [the goods given him]."[106]

4. Jāber b. Abdollāh al-Ansārī has related from the Most Noble Prophet: "At the end of time, a caliph will appear who will grant so much wealth that [its extent] will be beyond measure."[107]

---

[105] Eben Māja, Sonan, 2:1366-67, Hadith#4083; Hākem al-Haskānī an-Neyshāpurī, al-Mostadrak 'Alā's-Sahīhayn, 4:558; Borhān ol-Mottaqī, p. 81 (Chapter 1), Hadith#25 and p. 82 (Chapter 1), Hadith#26.

[106] Termedhī, Jame', 4:439 (Chapter 53) Hadith#2232; al-Ganjī ash-Shāfe'ī, Mohammad b. Yūsof b. Mohammad, al-Bayān fī Akhbār Sāheb oz-Zamān, p. 107 (Chapter 6); al-Elal ol-Motenāhīya, 2:858, Hadith#1440; Meshkāt ol-Masābīh, 3:24, Chapter 2, Hadith#5455; Eben Khaldūn, Moqaddama, p. 393 (Chapter 53); etc.

[107] Masābīh as-Sonnat, 3:488, Hadith#4199; also, there is an important hadīth report which appears in Abdor-Razzāq's Mosnaf (11:371, Hadith#20770) which is quoted by the author of Defā' an al-Kāfī (1:266).

5. Moslem b. al-Hajjāj reports in his Sahīh from Jāber b. Abdollāh al-Ansārī who has related from the Most Noble Prophet ﷺ: "At the end of time, a caliph will appear who will distribute countless wealth [among the community of Muslims]."[108]

9 The Miracles of Imām Mahdī

If Imām Mahdī ﷻ is one of the Immaculate Imāms, as the Shī'a believe, then he would necessarily have to be endowed with divine favors such as extra-ordinary knowledge and the ability to perform miracles in order to prove his imāmate (religio-political leadership) and the rightfulness of his succession to the Prophet ﷺ. His eleven ancestors before him were endowed with these attributes, and the hadīth reports which follow speak to these divinely-bestowed talents.

1. Alī b. Abī-Tāleb ﷺ has related that "The Mahdī will point to a bird in the sky and the bird will fall into his hands, and he will plant a dry staff into the ground and it will come alive and quickly sprout branches and leaves."[109]

2. Alī b. Abī-Tāleb ﷺ has also related that "Three banners will be unfurled; one in the Maghreb,[110] one in the Jazīra (Upper

---

[108] Moslem, Sahīh, in Nawawī's commentary on it, 18:39.
[109] Borhān ol-Mottaqī, p. 76 (Chapter 1), Hadith#14.
[110] Western North Africa: west of Egypt from Libya to Mauritania.

Mesopotamia), and the third in the Shām (the Levant). There will be war for a period of a year between them." [Imām Alī] then talks about the sedition of the Sofyānī[111] and his tyranny and oppression, and then about the advent of Imām Mahdī ﷻ and the pledging of allegiance of the people to him between the Rokn (Station) [of the Black Stone] and the Maqām (Station) [of Abraham],[112] [then continues,] "Imām Mahdī will move with his army steadily until he reaches the valley of Qorā.[113] At that point, his paternal cousin from the Hasanid line will join him with twelve thousand cavalry and tell him, 'O paternal cousin! I am more worthy than you of leading this army. I am the son of al-Hasan ﷺ and I am the Mahdī ﷻ.'

"Imām Mahdī ﷻ will respond, 'Rather, I am the Mahdī.'

"The paternal cousin from the Hasanid line will say, 'Do you have any sign by means of which I will be able to pledge allegiance to you?'

"Imām Mahdī ﷻ will point to a bird in the sky and the bird will fall into his hands. He will then take a piece of dry wood and plant it in the ground and it will come alive and quickly sprout branches and leaves. [At that point the paternal cousin from] the

---

[111] A leader of the forces of evil in the End Times.

[112] See footnote #66 on page 118.

[113] Northwest of Medina.

Hasanid [line] says, 'O paternal cousin! This cavalry is at your disposal!'"[114]

Summary and Conclusion

We discussed the fact that belief in a universal savior is not limited to the revealed religions but can also be seen in non-religious ideologies and worldviews. In addition to the belief of the communities who have faith in the revealed religions in the coming of a universal savior, scholarly research into the Old and New Testaments has determined that this awaited savior is none other than Imām Mahdī ﷻ. The religious scholars of the various confessional rites within Islam have made written avowals concerning the birth of the Mahdī that span from the year 260 of the Islamic calendar to the present.

Additionally, a glance at the compilations of hadīth reports with respect to Imām Mahdī ﷻ is sufficient for one to attain to certainty in the fact that these reports are *motewāter*;[115;116] and that the *tawātor* rank of these hadīth reports has been proven within the Sunni hadīth compilations which have been reported by Sunni scholars of the science of hadīth.[117]

---

[114] *Borhān ol-Mottaqī*, p. 76 (Chapter 1), Hadith#15.
[115] See footnote #7 on page 39.
[116] Cf. *Abrāz ol-Wahm ol-Maknūn*, p. 437.
[117] In his book al-Imām al-Mahdī (pages 259 to 365), Ostād Mohammad Alī Dakhīl lists thirty books written by Sunni scholars on this subject.

Many of the great religious scholars from among the ranks of the Sunnite confessions such as Termedhī (d. 297 Lunar); Hāfez Abū-Ja'far Aqīlī (d. 322 Lunar); Hākem al-Haskānī an-Neyshāpurī (d. 405 Lunar); Imām Beyhaqī (d. 458 Lunar); Imām Baghawī (d. 510 Lunar); Eben Athīr (d. 606 Lunar); Qartabī al-Mālekī (d. 671 Lunar); Eben Taymīya (d. 728 Lunar); Hāfez Dhahabī (d. 748 Lunar); Ganjī ash-Shāfe'ī (d. 658 Lunar); Hāfez Eben Qayyem (d. 751 Lunar);[118] have avowed to the veracity of the hadīth reports concerning Imām Mahdī ﷻ, and these avowals appear in their various writings.

Furthermore, a number of Sunni scholars have emphasized that the hadīth reports concerning Imām Mahdī ﷻ have reached the threshold of *tawātor* (i.e. that there can be no doubt about the soundness of the report); the list of these scholars includes: Barbahārī (d. 329 Lunar); Mohammad b. Hasan Ābarī ash-Shāfe'ī (d. 363 Lunar) – quoted by Qartabī al-Mālekī; also,

---

[118] Termedhī, Jame', 4:56, 4:505, 4:2230-31 and 4:2233.
Aqīlī, ad-Do'afā' ol-Kabīr, 3:253 and 3:1257. Hākem al-Haskānī an-Neyshāpurī, al-Mostadrak 'Alā's-Sahīhayn, 4:429, 4:465, 4:553, and 4:558. Beyhaqī, al-E'teqād wa'l-Hedāya ilā Sabīl ar-Rishād, p. 127. Hosayn b. Mas'ūd ash-Shāfe'ī (Farā' al-Baghawī), Masābīh as-Sonnat, 492 – 493, 4210, 4213, and 4215. Eben Athīr, an-Nahāya fī Gharīb ol-Hadīth wa'l-Athar, 5:254. Qartabī, at-Tadhkerat, p. 704. Eben Taymīya, Menhāj as-Sonnat an-Nabawīya, 4:211. Dhahabī, Talkhīs al-Mostadrak 'Alā's-Sahīhayn, 4:553 and 4:558. al-Ganjī ash-Shāfe'ī, Mohammad b. Yūsof b. Mohammad, al-Bayān fī Akhbār Sāheb oz-Zamān, p. 500. Eben Qayyem, al-Menār ol-Monīf, pages 130 to 135 and 326 to 331.

Qartabī al-Mālekī (d. 671 Lunar); Hāfez Jamāloddīn al-Mazanī (d. 742 Lunar); Hāfez Eben Qayyem (d. 751 Lunar); and Eben Hajar al-Asqalānī (d. 852 Lunar); etc. [119] Additionally, there are hadīth reports which confirm and lend further support to these *motewāter* reports, such as reports about the character, external appearances, and future actions of the Mahdī, as well as reports which discuss his name, honorific, the names of his father and mother, and the nobility of his lineage.

Thus, the applicability of the reports concerning which we have absolute certainty, (i.e. the *motewāter* reports) are bound by those reports which describe the Imām's characteristics and attributes, such as the following report: "He [the Imām al-Mahdī] is of the progeny of Abdol-Mottaleb and Abū-Tāleb and is a Member of the Household [of the Prophet], and is the offspring of the Apostle ﷺ of God ﷻ and of al-Hosayn ؑ and of Imām as-Sādeq ؑ and of Imām ar-Redā ؑ." And the sacred texts that specifically designate the Imām Mahdī ﷻ as the Caliph of God ﷻ and as the Final Imām, and which state that Jesus ؑ will defer to him to lead the communal prayers have specifically determined and designated His Eminence, and prove to us that he is the same person concerning whom the Prophet ﷺ gave the glad tidings of his advent, and who is none other than

---

[119] al-Ehtejāj bi'l-athar 'alā man Ankar al-Mahdī al-Montazer, p. 27. Qartabī, at-Tadhkeraᵗ, 1:7. Qartabī, at-Tadhkeraᵗ, 1:701. Tahdhīb al-Kamāl, 25:146. Eben Qayyem, al-Menār ol-Monīf, p. 130.

Mohammad b. Hasan al-Askarī ﷺ b. Ali al-Hādī ﷺ ... b. Alī b. Abī-Tāleb ﷺ.

Thus, it is now clear that the Mahdī was born in the second half of the third Islamic century and is currently alive and continues his life in a state that is occulted from normal vision.

The attention of the hadīth reports to his external appearances and to his character shows just how much attention the sacred law of Islam pays to the promised leadership of Imām Mahdī ﷻ, and how it is intent on determining true and verifiable criteria for the recognition of this promise. This is so as to preclude this covenant from becoming subject to abuse at the hands of charlatans and frauds. Additionally, the mentioning of these attributes and characteristics as prophecy has the added advantage of increasing people's confidence and faith in the Imām al-Mahdī ﷻ.

Islamic Messianism
By Abdol-Karīm Behbahānī

The Teachings of the Twelve Imāms are the Essence of Mahdism[120]

The belief in the advent of a universal savior of humanity, which is the essence of the belief in Islamic Mahdism (or Messianism), is a pervasive human belief which is not limited to a specific religion or denomination. This fact can dispense with four different misconceptions about Mahdism simultaneously:

1) The first false belief is the meme which states that Mahdism is a belief and expectation which is held exclusively by the Shī'a, and that the supposed "consensus" of the Muslim community is agreed on this.

2) The second false belief is the meme which states that Mahdism is nothing more than a myth, and that such myths are simple-minded fabrications which have their roots in national, tribal and

---

[120] Islamic messianism; the idea of the expectation of a universal savior for humanity.

clannish dynamics and social realities. However, there can be no such thing as a "myth" which all of the revealed religions as well as many non-religious ideologies and philosophies hold to in some way or another, and which furthermore, is a fact that is accepted by scientists, scholars and philosophers, and which on all of the above bases, is therefore an indicator of a felt presence in humanity's collective unconscious. This is not a mythical fabrication at all.

3) The third false belief is the meme which states that the Jews played a role in originating the idea of Mahdism. If the idea of Mahdism or the expectation of a universal savior for humanity is something that is prevalent in the revealed religions as well as in many non-religious ideological formations, then why should we not abide its reality within Islam as well, when reason demands that the mind should know about this idea more clearly and more completely, and especially in view of the fact that this is the belief of the Imāms of the *Ahl al-Bayt* (the Members of the Household of the Prophet ﷺ)?

Therefore, one of the signs of the perfection of the religion of Islam, and of the rite or denomination of the *Ahl al-Bayt* ﷺ in particular is that it should include the idea of Mahdism as an integral part of its beliefs. Is it not the case that the revealed religions hold many beliefs and practices in common, such as belief in angels and the hereafter, the obligation of performing ritual acts of devotion, etc.? Given this, does the fact that the Jewish religion or any another religion believes in these commonalities mean that Islam must therefore *not* believe in them? Or does it simply mean that if in fact our scriptural sources confirm such a belief to be part of our creedal principles, that Islam should, as with everything else, encompass the idea in its most progressed and perfected form? Thus, the assertion of such a spurious argument is in fact an indication of faulty logic and misconceived notions on the part of those who give expression to it; and it is an indication, on the other hand, of the perfection of Islam, and especially of Shī'a Islam in which this belief is fully elaborated.

4) The fourth false belief is the meme which states that belief in Mahdism springs from the political and social pressures which the followers of the school of the *Ahl al-Bayt* were subject to. To this objection we can respond by saying that the Khawārej, for example, were subject to a greater amount of such pressures, but they did not subscribe to this belief. Besides, if such social pressures and political repression causes this belief to arise, then at any moment where such pressures and repression exist, the subject repressed peoples and those who suffer oppression should therefore also hold messianic views; but this is not the case. And contrarily, the number of people who were not under the pressures of any such oppression and who nonetheless believe in the coming of a universal savior is very large indeed. Furthermore, if social pressures and political repression are the causes of Mahdism, then it would follow logically that when such pressures are lifted, that belief in the coming of a universal savior would concurrently or gradually disappear. But the reality belies this: the empirical evidence indicates that the opposite is the case, and that when the conditions of political oppression are lifted, the belief

in the coming of the Mahdī is made stronger and heightened in the following generations.

The only thing that can be asserted with certainty is that social and political pressures can be a *contributing or causal factor* for people to incline towards the belief in Mahdism, but not that these pressures are the *underlying principle and [ultimate] cause* of such beliefs. The fact is that religion is the more complete expression of the human condition, and Islam is the more complete expression of religion, and Shī'a Islam is the more complete expression of Islam. When the religions of the world emphasize the idea of the coming of a universal savior for mankind, what this in fact points to is an inner *fetric*[121] desire and need. And when Islam gives expression to this idea in a new and more perfected form compared to past religions, in addition to expressing a truth that is hidden from the normal faculties of human understanding, it emphasizes this basic *fetric* desire and need. When the Imāms of the *Ahl al-Bayt* emphasize and express this reality in greater detail, they are giving expression to this Islamic reality in a clearer and more perfected form.

Therefore, the difference between the School of the *Ahl al-Bayt*[122] and the School of the Caliphs[123] is that the latter expresses this

---

[121] Having to do with man's primordial disposition and orientation; with the way in which man has been created.
[122] Those who follow the Imāms from the Family of the Prophet, i.e. the Shī'a.
[123] Those who follow the caliphs, i.e. the Sunnis.

belief in a limited form while the former gives expression to it in a clearer, more expansive and more perfected form. This reality notwithstanding, some still believe that the School of the *Ahl al-Bayt* ﷺ have taken the path of exaggeration and extremism when it comes to the idea of the Mahdī! Perhaps the key to understanding the reputation of the School of the *Ahl al-Bayt* ﷺ concerning the issue of Mahdism, namely, the meme and false understanding that this belief belongs exclusively to the province of Shī'a beliefs and is not shared by the tradition of Sunni thought – perhaps the key to the disabuse of this false meme is attaining to the understanding that the *Ahl al-Bayt* ﷺ have raised the expression of this concept to the level of its perfection such that its expression has certain attributes that are unique to the Shī'a and are the expressions of the reality of Mahdism in its ideal and perfected form.

All of these attributes arise from a single wellspring, and that is the fact that from the perspective of the *Ahl al-Bayt* ﷺ, the messianic ideal is not simply a vision of the future that prophecies the felicity of humanity at the end of time – as is the case with the conception of the School of the Caliphs (Sunnīs) – but rather, it is an inseparable component of the beliefs of the Twelver Shī'a which has been decreed by Almighty God ﷻ – an idea that started with the passing of the Most Noble Prophet ﷺ and which will continue until the end of time. To put another way, the question of the imāmate (religio-political leadership) of the Twelfth Imām ﷺ began in the year 260 of the Islamic lunar calendar (the year of the beginning of the Lesser Occultation of the Twelfth Imām ﷻ), and continues to this day; and this imāmate will continue until the advent of the Twelfth Imām ﷻ at the end of time.

When we examine the issue of Mahdism from the vantage of the Ahl al-Bayt ﷺ, we must be cognizant of this creedal axis: our approach should be (1) the examination of the question as to whether or not this principle can be proven by means of rational proofs and the demanding logic of discursive arguments and/ or by means of scriptural proofs, (2) to survey the specific attributes associated with this belief, and (3) to evaluate the value and benefits of this belief. Thus, our investigation will proceed under the above three headings.

1 Proofs of the Belief in Mahdism

The proofs for the belief in the idea of a universal savior of humanity become crystal clear by way of hundreds of *hadīth* reports which have reached us[124] of the words of the Apostle ﷺ of God ﷻ which stipulate this savior to be the Imām al-Mahdī ﷻ and state that he is from the Family of the Prophet ﷺ of God ﷻ. These reports also tell us that he is of the progeny of Lady Fātema ﷻ, and is the ninth-generation progeny in the line

---

[124] Cf. *Ma'jam ol-Ahādīth al-Imām al-Mahdī*, Vol. 1: *Ahādīth an-Nabī*.

of Imām Hosayn[125] ؑ; and that the successors to the Prophet ﷺ shall be twelve in number.[126]

This group of five different types of *hadīth* reports expresses the identity of the Mahdī ﷻ as well as providing the scriptural bases for the belief in Mahdism, and anyone who studies these reports in any detail will notice that they gradually become more and more specific until they eventually focus on a specific individual.

In commenting on these *hadīth* reports, the martyr Sayyed Mohammad Bāqer as-Sadr states, "These reports have reached a high level of [reliability which comes from their having been reported by a large] multiplicity [of reliable narrators who have narrated these reports from various original sources]; and this is despite the fact that the Imāms ؑ had to resort to precautionary dissimulation (*taqīya*) in public in order to ensure the life and safety of the beloved Savior, and to preclude his becoming subject to the hostility of enemy forces."[127]

---

[125] For selections of various *hadīth* reports which justify all of the above claims, as well as references to their sources and many other sources, all of which are taken from Sunni books of *hadīth* compilations, refer to *chapter one*.

[126] For selections of various *hadīth* reports which provide the number of the successors of the Prophet ﷺ to be twelve, refer to *The True Origins and Teachings of Shī'a Islam*, forthcoming from Lantern Publications in 2021, God grant.

[127] Cf. Sadr, Mohammad Bāqer, *al-Ghayba' al-Kobrā*, p. 272 ff.

We hasten to add that the multiplicity of the *hadīth* reports is not the only criterion for accepting them as authentic. There are other reasons for believing these reports to be sound and well-founded. For example, take the noble *hadīth* report of the Prophet ﷺ which states that "There will be twelve caliphs (or, alternately, Imāms, or Emīrs) which will succeed me." Allowing for the variations in the text (shown in parentheses, above) which obtain within the different chains of transmission, this report has been reported over 270 times,[128] and it appears in the most authoritative books of both Sunni and Shī'a *hadīth* compilation, including the *Sahīhs* of Bokhārī[129] and Moslem,[130] Termedhī, Abū-Dāwūd, the *Masnad* of Ahmad b. Hanbal,[131] and the *Mostadrak Alā as-Sahīheyn* of Hākem-e Neyshabūrī.[132]

The important point to note here is that Bokhārī was a contemporary of the Imāms al-Jawād ؑ, al-Hādī ؑ, and of Imām Hasan al-Askarī ؑ. This fact is highly significant because it proves that this *hadīth* report was related and redacted from the

---

[128] *At-Tāj aj-Jāme' li'l-Osūl*, 3:40, where the author states that this report has been related by Bokhārī, Moslem and Termedhī, and refers the reader to the book *al-Imām al-Mahdī* written by Ali Mohammad Ali Dakhayyel for the details of the reports and their chains of narrators.

[129] Bokhārī, *Sahīh*, 9:101.

[130] *At-Tāj aj-Jāme' li'l-Osūl*, 3:40, where the author states that this report has been related by Bokhārī, Moslem and Termedhī. See also the *Sonan* of Abū-Dāwūd, 2:207.

[131] Ahmad b. Hanbal, *Mosnad*, 6:99, Hadith#20359.

[132] Hākem-e Neyshabūrī, *Mostadrak Alā Sahīheyn*, 3:618.

prophet at a time when the imāmate of all twelve Imāms had not as yet been actualized, which leaves no room for any doubt that the reporting of this *hadīth* gave expression to a reality that was to be realized at a later date in the persons of the Twelve Imāms ﷺ, as the fabricated *hadīth* reports which are attributed to the Prophet ﷺ are so attributed in order to justify events that have occurred in later periods and hence have not been recorded in *hadīth* texts. It is clear therefore that the *hadīth* reports relating to the Twelve-fold nature of the Imāmate did not refer to an externally-realized reality – as yet – but was an expression of a divine reality which was given voice to by the Most Noble Prophet ﷺ of whom the Noble Quran has said, [53:3-4] *nor does he speak out of his own desire: [all] that [which he conveys to you] is but [a divine] revelation with which he has been inspired*; and who said, "The caliphs that will succeed me shall be twelve in number."[133] The line of these Imāms ﷺ started with Imām Ali ﷺ and end with Imām Mahdī ﷺ, and this is the only rational interpretation of this noble prophetic *hadīth* report.

Moslem relates in his *Sahīh* by way of Qotayba^t b. Saī'd, who relates the report from Jāber b. Samara: "I went to visit the Prophet ﷺ with my father. I heard His Eminence say, 'This matter will not come to an end until twelve caliphs succeed me.' The Prophet ﷺ then said something else in a lower voice which I was not able to make out. I asked my father what he had said,

---

[133] Shaykh Saddūq, *al-Amālī*, p. 387.

and he said that the Prophet ﷺ said, 'All of them will be from [the tribe of] Quraysh.'"[134]

Moslem then relates this *hadīth* report from several other sources such that we see that in this authoritative compilation alone, it has been related by way of nine sources; and if we refer to other Sunni and Shī'a compilations, we will see that there it has been related through many chains of narration (*toroq*).[135]

The Bewilderment of the Sunnite Scholars in the face of this Hadīth Report and their Inability to Explain it.
Naturally, the question which arises concerning this famous *hadīth* report is: Who are these Twelve Successors?

Before we proceed to answer this question, let us state the possible ways in which it can conceivably be answered. It is clear that there are two possibilities here:

---

[134] Moslem, *Sahīh*, 6:03
[135] al-Bukhari, *as-Sahih*, 4:164 (Chapter XV of the *Kitab al-Ahkam*). Ahmad b. Hanbal, *al-Mosnad*, 1: 397, 5:86 and 6:94; Moslem, *al-Sahih*, 6: 2; Abu-Dāwud, *as-Sonan*, 4:106, Hadith#4279 & 4280; Tabarānī, *al-Ma'jam al-Kabīr*, 2:238 and 2:1996; Termedhī, *Jame'*, 4:501; Hākem al-Haskānī an-Neyshāpurī, *al-Mostadrak 'Alā's-Sahīhayn*, 3:618; Esfahānī, Ahmad b. Abdollāh, Abū-No'aym, *Helīat ol-Owlīā*, 4:333; Eben Hajr al-Asqalānī, *Fath ol-Bārī*, 13:211; Eben Kathīr, *al-Bidayah*, 6:245; al-Qunduzi, *Yanabi' al-Mawaddah*, p. 373; and dozens other sources.

1. It is possible that the intention of the Prophet ﷺ was to express the political realities of society which were to follow in his wake, just as there were numerous other prophecies issued by His Eminence ﷺ concerning other events, and this prophecy would similarly fall into this same category of prophecies, which we can refer to as "prophecies concerning the future."

2. It is possible that the intention of the Prophet ﷺ was declarative and that he wanted to issue a statement determining the succession and the twelve-fold nature of the leadership of the community that is to follow in his wake. Furthermore, that the substance of this declarative statement had to do with the nature of and the designation to succession of this leadership in accordance with the requirements of the revealed law (*sharī'a*) of Islam, and that it was not simply a prophecy which informs its audience of the future political realities of the Islamic community; and so, we can refer to this second possibility as a "creedal interpretation[136]" of the *hadīth* report.

A scholarly discussion demands that both possibilities be investigated, and that the one that is best supported by the scriptural and rational evidence and proofs is chosen. However, in so far as the followers of the School of the Caliphs are bound by their principle of the legitimacy of the reign of the caliphs, they have simply set aside the second possibility which is the thesis that the *hadīth* report is a form of designation. They have

---

[136] An interpretation having to do with the basic beliefs or first principles one has concerning one's religion.

erected their theological and juridical edifices on this (unstable) foundation! This is because in their limited view, they could only see one possibility; from which, what is more, they could not see a way out; thus, they proceeded to try to find explanations and rationalizations for other possibilities, even though these interpretations were all weak and led them far afield of anything that has any semblance of rationality. This is while their duty to the truth bound them to an unbiased examination of the subject *hadīth* report, the evaluation of which was to be free of any preconceived notions and judgments; in which case they would have reached the conclusion of the invalidity of the first possibility, i.e. that of the *hadīth* report being merely a "prophecy concerning the future."

Here we would like to pose the question to these gentlemen that if it were the case that the intention of the Most Noble Prophet ﷺ was to prophecy and express certain political realities which were to occur in the future, why would he limit the number of future caliphs to twelve when we know that more than this number came to power? Additionally, if it is said that the Most Noble Prophet ﷺ was referring to the caliphates of the legitimate caliphs whose reign was in conformance with the standards and norms of the sacred law, then it must be said that the followers of the School of the Caliphs have not reached consensus concerning the legitimacy of the reins of any of the caliphs other than the four "Rightly Guided" Caliphs; and that therefore, they have been bewildered and unable to come to any sort of consensus on the identity of the caliphs which supposedly constitute the twelve which the Most Noble Prophet had allegedly "prophesied" in the *hadīth* report.

For example, in Eben Kathīr's opinion, the twelve caliphs consist of, "... the four rightly-guided caliphs (Abū-Bakr, Omar, Othmān and Ali ﷺ), and then, Omar b. Abdol-Azīz [who] is [also] one of them; and some of the Abbāsid caliphs;" and it seems that he has posited the Mahdī to be one of these also!¹³⁷

And the Qādī ad-Dameshqī has stated, "These twelve people consist of the four rightly-guided caliphs, Mo'āwīya, Yazīd b. Mo'āwīya, Abdol-Mālek b. Marwān and his four sons: Walīd, Soleymān, Yazīd, and Hāshem, and the last one was Omar b. Abdol-Azīz."¹³⁸

In the opinion of Walīollāh al-Mohaddeth, as he has expressed it in his *Qorra' ol-'Aynayn* (and as quoted in *'Own al-Ma'būd*), these twelve caliphs consist of: "the four rightly-guided caliphs, Mo'āwīya, Abdol-Mālek b. Marwān and his four sons, Omar b. Abdol-Azīz, and Walīd b. Yazīd b. Abdol-Mālek." Walīollāh al-Mohaddeth then quotes Mālek b. Anas who includes Abdollāh b. Zobayr in this group, but then goes on to reject Mālek's position, stating, "It is related by Omar and Othmān from the Most Noble Prophet ﷺ that the reign of Abdollāh b. Zobayr is one of the great calamities which will befall this community."

---

¹³⁷ Eben Kathīr in his *Tafsīr al-Qorān al-Azīm*, 2:34, under the commentary of the 12ᵗʰ *āya* of the *Sūra' al-Māeda*.
¹³⁸ Qādī ad-Dameshqī, *Sharh al-Aqīda' at-Tahāwīya*, 2:736.

Walīollāh al-Mohaddeth then goes on to reject the position of those who have included Yazīd [b. Mo'āwīya] in the group of twelve, stating that "Yazīd was a depraved and notoriously [corrupt] person."[139]

Eben Qayyem al-Jowzayya has stated, "The successors of His Eminence ﷺ are twelve. A number of scholars including Abū-Hātam and Eben Habbān and others have stated that the last of them was Omar b. Abdol-Azīz, so that the order would be: the four Rightly Guided caliphs, Mo'āwīya, Yazīd b. Mo'āwīya, Mo'āwīya b. Yazīd, Marwān b. Hakam, Abdol-Mālek b. Marwān, Walīd b. Abdol-Mālek, Soleymān b. Abdol-Mālek, and then Omar b. Abdol-Azīz. Omar b. Abdol-Azīz died in the 100th year of the Islamic calendar, and this century was the best of centuries for the Islamic community and the religion enjoyed the heights of dignity and honor, after which the world of Islam was afflicted with all sorts of tribulations and calamities."[140]

Nūr-Bashtī states, "This *hadīth* report refers to caliphs who were of sound moral character, because it is only they who are truly worthy of being referred to as caliphs."[141]

Maqrīzī states: "They consist of the four Rightly Guided caliphs, and then Imām Hasan ﷺ, who brings [the cycle of] the rightly-

---

[139] *'Awn al-Mo'būd fī Sharh Sonan Abī-Dāwūd*, 11:246 (in the commentary on *Hadīth* #427).
[140] *Op cit.* 11:245.
[141] *Op cit.* 11:244.

guided caliphs to a close." Maqrīzī does not include any of the Omayyad caliphs in the group of twelve and states that the caliphate turned into a sultanate and kingship of oppression under which aegis much hardship was imposed on and borne by the people. Similarly, Maqrīzī does not include any of the Abbāsid caliphs in the group of twelve and states that "during their tenure, the unity of Islam unraveled, and the name of the Arabs was deleted from the roster (*dīwān*) [of the treasury] and the names of the Turks was established therein, and the Deylamīs and then the Turks ruled over the territories of Islam and formed large governorates, and the territories of Islam were subdivided, with each [contender] taking a portion of it [for themselves], and ruled over it by the force of arms."[142]

Given this state of affairs, the extent to which the followers of the caliphs have disagreed concerning the interpretation of this *hadīth* report can be seen, and how they have been immersed up to their necks in the quagmires and quicksand of the untenable acrobatics and gymnastics of bogus rationalizations, escape from which has been an impossibility for them for the simple reason that they have insisted upon the interpretation of the *hadīth* report based on the false understanding that it was of the nature of a "prophecy concerning the future."

---

[142] *As-Solūk lī Ma'rafa' Dowal al-Molūk*, 1:13-15 (Part 1).

Soyūtī writes, "To date, there have not been twelve caliphs identified upon whose [identity] the whole of the [scholarly] community of Islam has been able to reach a consensus."[143]

If the "prophecy concerning the future" interpretation of the *hadīth* report were correct, the Companions of the Prophet ﷺ would have been the first to interpret it in this way, and we would see the effect of such interpretations on their tongues immediately after the death of the Most Noble Prophet ﷺ, the first one saying, "*I* am the first of the twelve caliphs," and so on, these types of announcements being made through to the twelfth caliph, claiming this as an honor for themselves and a testament for the legitimacy of their respective reigns. History has not recorded a single instance of any such claim to this alleged prophesied chain.

Furthermore, it must be said that there is evidence from other *hadīth* reports which indicate that the length of the tenure of these twelve caliphs shall comprise the entirety of human history, and that at the end of their tenure, the earth will swallow up its inhabitants, as it appears in the following *hadīth* report as related in the Sunni sources: "This religion will remain in place while twelve people from [the tribe of] the Quraysh rule over it. After all of them leave the lower world (the *donyā*), the earth will swallow up its inhabitants."[144]

---

[143] *Al-Hāwī li'l-Fatāwī*, 2:85.
[144] Mottaqī al-Hendī, *Kanz ol-A'mmāl*, 12:34, Hadith#33861. (This report is related by Eben Najjār from [Mālek b.] Anas.)

Islamic Messianism

It might come as a surprise to some to find that after the reign of Omar b. Abdol-Azīz, the earth did *not* in fact swallow up its inhabitants, but that rather, the Quranic sciences such as jurisprudence (*feqh*), *hadīth* science, and Quranic commentary and exegesis (*tafsīr*) flourished in the third and fourth centuries and bloomed after the death of the "twelve caliphs" (from the perspective of the followers of the School of the Caliphs), whereas their assumption was that the earth would swallow up its inhabitants after the death of the last caliph in their supposed series of twelve.

It is also related from Jāber b. Samara that "The affairs of this community will remain in place and will be victorious over its enemies until twelve caliphs, all of whom are from [the tribe of] the Quraysh, shall rule, after which chaos will ensue and will encompass the world."[145]

If what is meant by "chaos" is repression and oppression, then it must be said that the Islamic community has not seen a greater sedition and act of treachery than Mo'āwīya's revolution against the caliph of the Muslim believers. This fact is sufficient reason to believe that the "chaos" referred to here is something that is larger even than that which Mo'āwīya inflicted upon the community, and that perhaps what is meant is a time when the religion itself is set aside altogether. This is something that will not occur except at the approach of the end of days and the Resurrection, at which time Imām Mahdī ﷻ will appear, and

---

[145] Mottaqī al-Hendī, *Kanz ol-A'mmāl*, 12:32, Hadith#33848.

after the passage of certain incidents and events, will be martyred and will return to his Maker.

Here we must ask those who follow the School of the Caliphs (i.e. our Sunni brethren) what sense there is in including the sultans and kings who instituted and perpetuated dynastic rule in the list of the twelve-fold caliphs which the Prophet ﷺ referred to? The following *hadīth* report appears in the Sunni compilations of *hadīth* from Sa'd b. Abī-Waqqās who was one of the "Ten Evangelists" and was one of the members of the council which Omar b. al-Khattāb appointed to determine the identity of his successor. The *hadīth* report relates that Sa'd b. Abī-Waqqās entered into Mo'āwīya's presence while he had refrained from pledging allegiance to him. After entering, Sa'd said, "Greetings to you, O King!" Mo'āwīya said, "Could you not come up with anything other than this [greeting]?? You are a believer and I am your Emir!" Sa'd said, "That would have been true if we had made you our Emir!" In another version of the same report it appears as follows: "We are believers, but have not appointed you as our Emir!" Āesha also denied the legitimacy of Mo'āwīya's caliphate, just as Eben Abbās and Imām Hasan ؑ denied him any legitimacy whatsoever even after the signing of the armistice.[146]

Mo'āwīya was a seditionist and a revolutionary according to a broad consensus, and the Prophet ﷺ has stated in a *hadīth* report: "O Ammār! You will be martyred by a group of

---

[146] Amīnī, Allāme, *al-Ghadīr*, 1:26-27.

mutineers." All this notwithstanding, it is difficult for us to fathom how some have considered (and still consider!) such a mutineer to be the legitimate successor of the Most Noble Prophet ﷺ!?

The question must also be posed as to what possible sense can there be in including Yazīd in the list of these twelve caliphs?? Was it not the case that he was a lecher and a corrupt debauchee and an open drunkard?! How can a Muslim in good conscience consider such a lecher who is notorious for the murder of the grandson of the Prophet ﷺ at the plain of Karbalā, and for the atrocities that followed in the city of Medina where tens of thousands of Muslims were put to death – how can such a devil be considered the lawful successor of the Apostle ﷺ of God?

This same question can be posed with respect to The Accursed Tree of the Omayyads which the Quran has referred to,[147] and which the Apostle ﷺ of God ﷻ saw in a vision that "the Banī-Omayya will rise up to their pulpits like monkeys", and this is something that most of the Sunni exegetes of the Quran point to in their commentaries on *āya* sixty of the *Sūraʾ ol-Esrā*, so that there is no need to cite each of them individually.

We can draw three conclusions from the above clarifications.

---

[147] Reference to 17:60.

1. The position which considers the *hadīth* report of the twelve caliphs of the Quraysh to be a "prophecy of the future" is null and false.

2. Political considerations have been a major causal factor for the followers of the caliphs to be drawn to this interpretation.

3. The true and legitimate interpretation of this *hadīth* report can only be attained by way of the alternate "creedal interpretation" of the report which maintains that the prophetic statement was stipulative, and that it affirms the fact that the twelve successors were appointed by God ﷻ. This interpretation is affirmed by way of rational and scriptural proofs that can be found in both the Quranic revelations and in the prophetic *hadīth* corpus, and extensive arguments in its favor have been presented in the fields of Quranic exegesis (*tafsīr*), *hadīth* science, dogmatic or creedal theology (*kalām*), and history.

History teaches us that the Twelve Imāms of the Ahl al-Bayt ﷺ (the Members of the Household of the Prophet) are the only possible true and proper application of the *hadīth* report of the Prophet ﷺ – an appropriateness which no one disputes, even at the level of a claim or assertion. The first of these Imāms is Alī b. Abī-Tāleb ؑ and the last of them is His Eminence the Imām al-Mahdī ﷼; and there are numerous *hadīth* reports concerning this topic, one of which we shall refer to presently.

The Shāfe'ī scholar Jowaynī reports in his *Farāed as-Samtayn* from Eben Abbās, who relates that the Most Noble Prophet ﷺ said, "I am the master (*seyyed*) of the prophets and Alī b. Abī-Tāleb ؏ is the master of the *wasī'īn* (plural of *wasī*: inheritor, successor, legatee, executor); and my successors shall be twelve [in number], the first of whom is Alī b. Abī-Tāleb ؏ and the last of whom shall be the Mahdī."[148]

Based on this *hadīth* report, certain scholars[149] have posited the possibility that the report in which some of the words of the Most Noble Prophet ﷺ are reported to have remained obscure to Jāber b. Samara[150] (where Jāber is related not to have heard something that the Prophet ﷺ said and was informed by his father that he said that "they will all be of [the tribe of] the Quraysh") might in fact be an example of *hadīth* report distortion. This is because the report states the reason for this portion of the speech of the Prophet ﷺ having become obscure to Jāber as being the ruckus raised by the people and their wailing and yawling and hollering; whereas these expressions of emotion are not appropriate to or are a disproportionate response to the words which Jāber is reported not to have heard (and which we are made privy to by way of his father, namely, that "they will all be of [the tribe of] the Quraysh"), because stipulating the caliphate to be contained

---

[148] Jowaynī, *Farāed as-Samtayn*, 2:313, Hadith#564.
[149] Cf. Āmelī, Seyyed Ja'far Mortaḍā, *al-Ghadīr wa'l-Mo'āreḍūn*, pgs. 70 - 77.
[150] See page 149 above, and Moslem, *Sahīh*, 6:03.

within the domain of the Quraysh is something that would have gladdened them, and would not have been the cause of their wailing and moaning and disrupting the meeting session.

Rather, what would be the more appropriate catalyst for such emotional outbursts and such a disruption would have been the stipulation of the succession and the imāmate (the religio-political leadership of the community) to a special group *other* than the Quraysh; and this is exactly what the 13th century Lunar Hanafī scholar Qondūzī has related in his *Yanābī' ol-Mowadda*, where he relates that the expression the Most Noble Prophet uttered was the following: "they will all be of [the clan of] the Banī-Hāshem."[151]

❖

We have now reached the stage where on one hand we have proven the falsity of the interpretation of the famous *hadīth* report of the twelve caliphs as being of the type that "prophesy future events," and on the other hand we have established the veracity of the "creedal interpretation" of this report. Additionally, we elucidated the fact that the name of Imām Mahdī appears in the list of names in the series of twelve caliphs or Imāms, and that God will fill the world with justice and equity by means of him, after it will have become filled with injustice and

---

[151] That is the clan of the Prophet; cf. Qondūzī, *Yanābī' ol-Mowadda*, 3:104 (Chapter 77).

oppression. Therefore, there is no longer any room for doubt concerning the adoption of the specific definition of Mahdism which the *Ahl al-Bayt* ﷺ have insisted upon.

The deep interconnectedness of the subject of Mahdism with the question of the succession of the Twelve Imāms leads us to say that the interpretation of the *hadīth* report of the twelve caliphs as being of the type that "prophesy future events" has no bearing on the stipulation and appointment of the Most Noble Prophet ﷺ of his twelve successors, and that it has been the interference of political considerations and dynamics which has caused those who follow the caliphs to resort to such interpretations, and to neglect the "creedal interpretation" which considers the matter of the succession and the imāmate or religio-political leadership of the community to be a matter of divine designation. In fact, we can say that those who follow the caliphs interpreted this seminal *hadīth* report as one which was simply a prophecy of future events in order for them to be able to rationalize and justify the events of the Saqīfa[152] and to be able to legitimize the tripartite caliphates of Abū-Bakr, Omar and Othmān. Consequent to the error of this interpretative pathway which they perforce had to

---

[152] The Saqīfa was a portico of the Banī Sā'eda where the Ansār (the clans of Yathreb/Medina who had entered into Islam and were its "Helpers") had gathered immediately upon the death of the Prophet ﷺ in order to determine who was to rule their city. It became the scene of the first manifestation of a carefully planned plot according to which six chieftains of Quraysh were to succeed, one after another, in taking the reins of leadership of the community after the Prophet's passing.

take as a consequence of decisions which were rooted in their political allegiances, they were similarly obliged to interpret the issue of Mahdism or the coming of a universal savior for mankind purely as a prophecy of some abstract future event and nothing more, i.e. it was a messianism divorced from the historical person which was referred to repeatedly in the prophetic *hadīth* corpus, so that by interpreting the *hadīth* reports relating to the Mahdī and Mahdism in such abstract and general terms, they could evade the duty of accepting, pledging allegiance to, and obeying the Twelve Imāms stipulated by the Prophet ﷺ. This is because the acceptance of the veracity and truth of the creedal interpretation of the *hadīth* of the twelve caliphs necessarily entails and is concomitant with the proof of the legitimacy and truth of the creedal concept of Mahdism (as interpreted by the Shī'a and which applies to the leadership of a specific person from the Family of the Prophet ﷺ) – and this is something which they were wont to escape from and refuse to be bound to – a reference which has been sustained even unto the present day.

2 The Specific Attributes of the Definition of Mahdism from the Perspective of the Ahl al-Bayt

Having established the proof of the "creedal interpretation" for the issue of Mahdism from the point of view of the *Ahl al-Bayt* ﷺ, we can now enter a new stage, which is the examination of the specific attributes relative to this topic.

Our intention is to establish the fact that these attributes are real, are a definite part of that which has been revealed by God, have been realized historically, and that attaining to faith in them is not at variance with any Islamic first principle or with any historical realities. These specifics are as follows:

1. The Covert Birth of the Imām al-Mahdī

With the establishment of the proof of the "creedal interpretation" for the issue of Mahdism from the point of view of the *Ahl al-Bayt*, and the fact that the Mahdī is an actual person who is from the progeny of the Prophet who was born to the Eleventh Imām in the line of the Twelve Imāms, it becomes evident that the most immediate necessity which follows from this understanding is that the birth of the Twelfth Imām had to have taken place in covert circumstances, so that the occultation can take place shortly thereafter. Being hidden from view and being occulted to a place chosen by God is on account of the fact that the Twelfth Imām is the last star in the firmament of the Imāmate, and he will remain in a state of occultation until such a time as God deems appropriate; and what this divine wisdom necessarily entails is that the Twelfth Imām have a covert birth and a long life which is hidden from the view of others, so that the twelfth proof (*hojja*) [153] of God remain on earth, even if he is hidden from view and is in a state of occultation.

---

[153] The perfect embodiment and clear evidence of all truth on Earth and the conclusive argument and evidentiary proof against all falsehood on Judgement Day.

Given this understanding, the questions as to why the birth of the Twelfth Imām ﷻ occurred in secret and why his existence was not evident to the general public (so that it could easily be verified) no longer arise. This is because if this were not the case, the occultation would necessarily be precluded, which in turn would mean that the number of Imāms would have to exceed twelve, which would conflict with the prophetic *hadīth* report. Thus, the covert birth of the Twelfth Imām ﷻ is a fact that is implicit in, and necessarily follows from, the logic and implications of the prophetic *hadīth* reports.

These matters make it clear that proving a matter such as the birth of the Imām al-Mahdī and the reality of his life as an objective fact is not possible under the auspices of discussions that are limited purely to historical considerations, especially when one considers the fact that this matter had to, out of necessity to be shrouded in secrecy from the very beginning. Rather, this is a compound subject that involves creedal as well as historical considerations, and in which, what is more, creedal considerations play the predominant role, and in which the historical narrative acts as a supplement to some extent. Due to the political persecution of the Ālid line under the Omayyads and Abbāsids, the nature of the historical narrative was such that only a very few specially selected partisans of the House of the Prophet were privy to these events. Thus, if the people who lived contemporaneously with these events and were even present in the geographical vicinities in which they occurred were to be asked about them, they would either plead ignorance or deny that any such events had taken place.

We must be cognizant of the fact that we are not talking about a tangible event, nor one which was overt to the senses which could be recorded in all its details in the annals of history so that we can prove or disprove its objective reality or the fact of whether such a record even exists. Rather, the subject of our discussion is a truth which has reached us by way of prophetic *hadīth* reports from the Most Noble Prophet ﷺ and by way of reports from the Immaculate Imāms ؑ, all of whom have provided us with information from sources of knowledge which are beyond the ken of ordinary human perception or to the ordinary faculties of the senses; so that we are perforce obliged to be content with using whatever historical evidence that *does* exist as *secondary* proofs of a reality which has been established for us by way of scripture.

The *hadīth* reports of certain select individuals who have provided testimony concerning the birth and life of the Imām Mahdī ؑ, as well as his entering into a state of Minor Occultation, and later, into the Greater Occultation, are relevant cases in point, some of which we shall mention presently.

1.1 The Testimony of Imām Hasan al-Askarī

The testimony of Imām Hasan al-Askarī ؑ to the birth of his son, Imām Mahdī ؑ is related by Mohammad b. Yahyā, who relates the report from Ahmad b. Eshāq, from Abū-Hāshem al-Ja'farī, who said: "I told Abū-Mohammad [Imām Hasan al-Askarī ؑ]:

'Your solemnity and dignity prevent me from being able to ask you a question; will you permit me to do so?'

He said, 'Ask what you will.' And I said, "O my master! Do you have any children?' He said, 'Yes.'"[154]

This *hadīth* report is flawless and perfect in terms both of its provenance title (*sanad*) and in terms of the conformity of its content to the other Quranic and scriptural sources and the rational probative criteria used in the science of *hadīth*. The narrator, Mohammad b. Yahyā Abū-Ja'far al-Attār al-Qomī is one of the greats among the Shī'a to whose shrine pilgrimage is still made to the present day, and the books of personalities (*rejāl*) provide testamentary evidence as to the respect which Imām Hasan al-Askarī ؏ had for Ahmad b. Eshāq, as they do as well to the rank and station of Dāwūd b. Qāsem b. Eshāq b. Abdollāh b. Ja'far b. Abū-Tāleb, Abū-Hāshem al-Ja'farī. Additionally, attention should be paid to the fact that there are only two intermediaries in the chain of custody of this *hadīth* report, which means that its provenance title is proximate [to the original source] (i.e. it is *qorb ol-asnād*), which is an important consideration in ascertaining the veracity of a given report.

1.2 The Testimony of Lady Qābala.

Lady Qābala was the sister of Imām Hādī ؏, and the aunt of Imām Hasan al-Askarī ؏, and the daughter of Imām Jawād ؏,

---

[154] Koleynī, Shaykh Mohammad b. Ya'qūb, Theqat ol-Islam, *Osūl al-Kāfī*, 1:328.

has provided testimony concerning the birth of Imām Mahdī ﷻ.¹⁵⁵ She was the midwife of Narjes (Imām Mahdī's mother) on the night of the nativity.¹⁵⁶

1.3 The Testimony of Others about their Seeing Imām Mahdī

Our historical sources provide a long list of people who have seen Imām Mahdī ﷻ. Some scholars have compiled these names in books written specifically for this purpose, such as the book *Tabseraʿ ol-Walī fī man raʾy al-Qāem al-Mahdī* by Sayyed Hāshem al-Bahrānī, in which the names of 79 people are listed who have testified to seeing the Imām Mahdī ﷻ during his childhood and/ or during the period of the Lesser Occultation (260 to 329 Lunar), and which also provides the names of the sources upon which he has relied.

Shaykh Abū-Tāleb Tajlīl at-Tabrīzī has listed the names of 304 people who have testified to seeing the Imām Mahdī ﷻ.¹⁵⁷ And Shaykh Saddūq (d. 381 Lunar) has named 64 people who have testified to seeing the Imām Mahdī ﷻ, many of whom were the representatives of the Imām in various towns.¹⁵⁸ Among the representatives who have seen the Imām are the following:

---

¹⁵⁵ Koleynī, Shaykh Mohammad b. Yaʾqūb, Theqat ol-Islam, *Osūl al-Kāfī*, 1:330.

¹⁵⁶ *Kamāl od-Dīn*, 2:424 (Chpater 42).

¹⁵⁷ Shaykh Abū-Tāleb Tajlīl at-Tabrīzī, *Man Hūa al-Mahdī?*, pgs. 460 – 506.

¹⁵⁸ *Kamāl od-Dīn*, 2:442 (Chpater 43); Majlesī, Allame Mohammad Bāqer, *Behār ol-Anwār*, 52:30 (Chapter 26).

From Azarbāyjān: Qāsem b. 'Alā'. From Ahwāz: Mohammad b. Ebrāhīm b. Mahzīār. From Baghdād: Hajez al-Balālī; Othmān b. Saī'd al-Omarī; Mohammad b. Othmān b. Saī'd al-Omarī; and Attār. From Kūfa: 'Āsemī. From Qom: Ahmad b. Eshāq; From Neyshabūr: Mohammad b. Shādhān. From Hamadān: Basāmī; Mohammad b. Abī-Abdollāh al-Kūfī al-Asadī; and Mohammad b. as-Sāleh. The book goes on to list several dozen people who had testified to seeing the Imām but who were not his representatives.

Given all this historical evidence (on top of the irrefutable scriptural evidence by way of prophetic *hadīth* reports), does it make sense to deny the Imām's birth when this would mean that one would have to subscribe to a theory that posits a conspiracy between all these people to lie in unison about this one event? Bear in mind that the books of personalities (*rejāl*) in the science of *hadīth* have certified many of these people to be of sound moral character and to be people whose testimony can be relied upon.

1.4 The Reaction of the Abbāsid ruling Powers to this Event.

After the martyrdom of Imām Hasan al-Askarī, the tyrannical Abbāsid ruling power treated his family in such a way that it was evident that they feared the child whose birth (and whereabouts) they had not been privy to and concerning which they were left unawares. They therefore put all their resources into searching for him so that perhaps they might find and kill him. The Abbāsid caliph al-Mo'tamed (d. 279 Lunar), for example, ordered his forces to do a thorough search of Imām Hasan al-Askarī's house and to place it under surveillance, and ordered the bondsmaidens of Abū-Mohammad (Imām Hasan al-Askarī ﷺ) to be taken into custody and ordered his wives to be kept under surveillance. It is reported that the Imām's brother, Ja'far the Liar, cooperated with the authorities in this operation. Thus, the House of Imām Hasan al-Askarī ﷺ was subject to all sorts of harassment and punitive measures; some of them were detained temporarily, some were imprisoned, and others were sent into exile.[159]

All these events occurred when Imām Mahdī ﷺ was five years old. But for the Abbāsid caliph al-Mo'tamed, his age was not important; for he well understood that this child was destined to overthrow the throne and crown of his illegitimate and tyrannical reign, because the *hadīth* report from the prophet was well-known wherein he had said that the Twelfth Imām from the *Ahl al-Bayt* of the Prophet will fill the world with equity and justice after it has become filled with inequity and injustice. Al-Mo'tamed's stance with respect to the Imām al-Mahdī was the same stance that Pharaoh took against Moses ﷺ, whose mother released his cot on the river Nile for fear of Pharaoh's forces.

Of course, al-Mo'tamed was not the only king that had understood this matter; rather, the kings before him such as al-Mo'taz and al-Mo'tadī were aware of this matter also, which is why Imām Hasan al-Askarī ﷺ took the greatest precautions to prevent the dissemination of the news of the birth of Imām

---

[159] Mofīd, Shaykh, *al-Ershād*, 2:336.

Mahdī ﷻ and to ensure that only a select group of people should become aware of it.

If the scholars of the School of the Caliphs have not understood this, the Omayyad and Abbāsid sultans assuredly understood that the description of the Twelve Imāms which appears in the *hadīth* report of Jāber b. Samara did not apply to them, and that its only true and proper application was to the Members of the Household of the Prophet ﷺ, which is why they greatly feared the Twelfth Imām ﷻ. This is the only rational reason that can be provided for their fear of a five-year-old child and for the measures they took to try to find him. They believed that this child was the "Awaited Mahdī" concerning whom *motewāter*[160] *hadīth* reports had given glad tidings. This is why they detained Imām Hasan al-Askarī's bondsmaidens and had midwives inspect them lest they be pregnant with child. They even kept some of these bondsmaidens under surveillance for a period of two years, while the house of Imām Hasan al-Askarī ؑ was also constantly kept under surveillance, and spies were appointed to monitor the goings on in the household and to report back their findings.

❖

---

[160] A *motewāter hadīth* report is one that is transmitted with such frequency through different chains of narrators in exactly the same way to the extent that there can remain no doubt concerning the authenticity and reliability of the text in question. Cf. footnote #7 on page 39 also.

The question arises at this juncture as to why the ruling powers did not accept the word of Ja'far the Liar[161] who said that his brother had died and had not left any issue behind? Was it not easier for them to delegate the estate of Imām Hasan al-Askarī to his brother Ja'far the Liar and to cease their persecution of the House of the Prophet? It might be objected that the Abbāsid sultan wanted to find other people who would have inherited from the death of Imām Hasan al-Askarī and to distribute their due from the estate in accordance with the sacred law of Islam, so that Ja'far the Liar would not be its sole beneficiary based on his own testimony! In response we say that it was beneath the dignity of such a government to get involved with such petty investigations, and that the duty of the Abbāsids was to refer the matter of the claim of Ja'far the Liar to a court of law so that a qādī (judge) could make the necessary determinations concerning the disbursement of the estate, for in these circumstances, the qādī could summon such witnesses as the paternal aunt, mother, and bondsmaidens of the Imām and other of his relatives from the Banī-Hāshem and hear their

---

[161] Ja'far, generally known as 'the Liar' (*al-kaddhāb*), was the son of Imam Ali an-Naqī and the brother of Imam Hasan al-Askarī. Since he claimed the Imamate against Imam Mahdī, Shī'a biographers refer to him as 'the Liar'. There is a hadith report attributed to Imam Mahdī regarding Ja'far the Liar that likens him to the brothers of the prophet Joseph. Tabarsī and some other scholars are of the view that Ja'far repented like Joseph's brothers did, and that he came to be known as Ja'far at-Tawwāb (Ja'far the Penitent) after his repentance.

testimony as well as that of the plaintiff before issuing his verdict and putting an end to the matter.

But the report of this affair expressly states that the matter [of the estate] was referred to the highest authority of the land before Imām Hasan al-Askarī ﷺ had been buried. The taking of this matter out of the hands of the courts and the continued surveillance and persecution of the House of the Prophet ﷺ clearly demonstrates that the Abbāsid authorities were certain that the promised Mahdī was the last in the series of the Twelve Imāms of the Members of the Household of the Prophet ﷺ. This belief was reinforced by another *motewāter hadīth* report which states that "These two – the Quran and my Family – will not part company from each other until they come into my presence at the Pond of Kowsar [in Heaven];" so that if the Mahdī had *not* been born, or if his life had not been prolonged beyond the normal and natural lifespan of the average human life, either one of these possibilities would lead to the discontinuity of the Family of the Prophet ﷺ, which in turn would mean that the Lesser Trust[162] would become extinct. This

---

[162] This refers to the Hadīth of the Two Weighty Trusts, where the Prophet ﷺ is reported to have said in various places (the following text is from the version of his farewell sermon which was delivered at Ghadīr Khomm: "O ye people, I will precede you [to the next world] and you will enter into my presence at the Pond of Kowthar, a pond whose width is [equal to] the length of the distance from Basrī to San،ā , around which are arrayed silver goblets, countless as the starts of the night sky; and [at that time], I shall ask [each of] you concerning the Two

is something that none of the Abbāsid sultans who – absurdly – considered themselves to be the caliphs of the Muslims, could accept.[163]

Weighty Trusts [= the two things of high value,] which I left amongst you in trust. So pay attention to how you treat these two after I have departed!"

Here someone cried out, "O Prophet of God! What are those two things of value?" And the Prophet responded, "The first is the Book of God ﷻ one end of which is in God's hands and the other in yours. Keep it well and obey its decrees and do not allow any change to enter into it, for you will [surely] go astray [if you do]. And the other is my Family (*etratī*), the Members of my House (*ahl al-baytī*), and Almighty God ﷻ has informed me that these two shall never be parted until they enter into my presence at the Pond of Kowthar – this I have asked of my Lord. Therefore, do not surpass these two, if you are to be saved from perdition, and do not fall behind from them, for you will be annihilated. Do not [attempt to] teach them anything, as they are more knowledgeable than you." Some *hadīth* reports state that Apostle ﷺ of God ﷻ said, "As long as you hold fast unto these two [Trusts], you will not go astray." Cf. Hākem al-Haskānī an-Neyshāpurī, *al-mostadrak fī sahīhayn*, 3:109 & 3:533 (Dhahabī has concurred with Hākem's ruling that this hadīth is sahīh in his *talkhīs* (summarization) of the *mostadrak*. Also see, Ahmad b. Hanbal, *masnad*, 5:181-189; Termedhī, *Jame'*, 2:308 & 5:328 Hadith#3874; Nasāī, *Khasāes Amīr al-Mo'menīn*, p. 21; Mottaqī al-Hendī, *Kanz ol-A'māl*, 1:44 & 1:47-48; Moslem, *sahīh*, In the chapter on the virtues of Ali ؑ; Dāramī, *sonan*, 2:431; Eben-Sa'd, *Tabaqāt al-Kobrā*, 2:2; Monāwī's *konuz ol-haqāeq*, 3:14; *Heliat ol-Owliā*, 1:355, Hadith#64; Heythamī, *Majma' oz-Zawāed*, 9:163-164.

[163] *Defā' an al-Kāfī*, 1:567-8.

1.5 The Avowal of the Sunnī Olamā to the Birth of Imām Mahdī

If one refers to the book *Elzām on-Nāseb*, one will find the words of 29 Sunnī *olamā* (scholars of religion) quoted which come to over one hundred pages in which these scholars have avowed their belief that the Mahdī has already been born.[164] Perhaps the most comprehensive Shī'a book in this field is *al-Mahdī al-Montazer fī Nahj ol-Balāgha* by Ayatollāh Mahdī Faqīhī-e Īmānī, in which the author cites the names of 102 Sunnī scholars who have avowed the birth of Imām Mahdī ﷻ.[165] This list of 102 Sunnī scholars does not include another 30 which are not included therein but have been cited in various other books on the subject.[166]

Thāmer 'Amīdī has compiled these avowals in chronological order to manifest more fully the consensus of the Sunnī scholars concerning their avowal to the birth of Imām Mahdī ﷻ.[167] 'Amīdī then proceeds to list a bibliography consisting of 128 books written by Sunnī scholars in which the phrase "the twelfth

---

[164] Hāerī Yazdī, Ayatollāh Alī, *Elzām an-Nāseb fī Ethbāt al-Hojja' al-Ghā'eb*, 1:321-440.

[165] Faqīhī Īmānī, Ayatollā Mahdī, *al-Mahdī al-Montazer fī Nahj ol-Balāgha*, pages 16 – 30.

[166] Mūsawī, Seyyed Mohammad Saī'd, *Al-Imām ath-Thānī Ashar*, pages 27 – 70, where the author cites the names of thirty other Sunni olamā in the margins of the book on pages 89 – 93. See also Askarī, Shaykh Najmoddīn, *al-Mahdī al-Mowūd al-Montazer 'and Ahl as-Sonna was al-Imāma*, 1:220-226.

[167] *Defā' an al-Kāfī*, 1:568.

Imām from the [line of] Imāms of the *Ahl al-Bayt* ﷺ" appear in their texts.[168]

Among these scholars are some who lived during the time of the birth of His Eminence ﷻ and during the time of his Lesser Occultation. The testimony of these scholars has extraordinary value in terms of the historical documentation of this reality. Some of these personages include:

> 1. Abū-Bakr Rowyānī, Mohammad b. Hārūn (d. 307 Lunar) in the book *al-Masnad*.
>
> 2. Ahmad b. Ebrāhīm b. Alī al-Kendī (d. 310 Lunar), one of the students of Jarīr at-Tabarī.
>
> 3. Mohammad b. Ahmad b. Abī-Thalaj, Abū-Bakr al-Baghdādī (d. 322 Lunar), in the book *Mawālīd ol-A'emma*.

Another scholar who lived close to the era of the Lesser Occultation and who is considered to be one of the great scholars of the Sunnī rite is Khārazmī (d. 378 Lunar) who points to the birth of the Imām al-Mahdī ﷻ in his book *Mafātīh ol-Olūm* (pages 32 to 33 of the 1895 Leiden edition).

---

[168] Ibid.

1.6 Deniers of the Birth of Imām Mahdī

Among the subjects which deniers of the birth of Imām Mahdī ﷻ have resorted to are the differences within Shīʿa *hadīth* reports concerning the date of his birth and concerning his name, as well as the testimony of Jaʿfar the Liar, the paternal uncle of the Imām al-Mahdī ﷻ, to the effect that his brother left the world without leaving behind any issue. We respond to these claims by saying firstly that the historical method does not have efficacy for proving or disproving something that is held as a matter of faith and as a creedal belief and to which faith is attained by way of scriptural as opposed to rational or historical or empirical proofs; and which, furthermore, pertains in some of its elements to the world that is beyond the ken of ordinary human perception – in such cases, the ambit of the efficacy of the application of historical facts is limited to their function as supplementary confirming data. Furthermore, as has already been explained above, the entirety of the argument is premised on the furtive and covert nature of the birth of the Imām ﷻ based on the need to protect him from being found by enemy forces. If one grants these premises (which are indeed verifiable historical facts that are not in dispute), then the fact that the year of the birth was shrouded in secrecy or other factors such as variations in reports concerning the name of the mother of the Imām and so on follow naturally and are to be expected; because Imām Hasan al-Askarī's ؑ intention was to keep this event secret even from those closest to him, in order to preclude even the possibility of news of it reaching the Abbāsid authorities and court. Thus, the claim of Jaʿfar the Liar that Imām Hasan al-Askarī ؑ left the world without leaving behind any issue is such a case in point. Even if we assume for the sake of the argument that he was a truthful person, such a claim can easily be explained away, let alone the fact that the report is the testimony of someone who was infamous as a liar and a debauchee whose testimony can never be cited as a reliable source of reference.[169]

2. Investiture to the Imāmate during Childhood

Among the other attributes specific to Imām Mahdī ﷻ is his being vested with the office of the imāmate (the religio-political leadership of the community) while still a child and not yet having reached the age of majority. The response to this issue can be approached in one of two ways. It can be approached from the perspective of faith with a view to respond to the misunderstandings which people have about the subject; or, it can be approached from a desire to arrive at a truth [whose derivation is independent of scriptural sources and proofs], which involves research into the question as to whether the imāmate (of a five-year old child) is real in the sense of whether the occupant of the office of the imāmate is capable of embodying the qualifications necessary properly to carry out the functions of the religio-legal leadership of the community of the faithful – or whether this is merely an empty claim.

---

[169] Koleynī, Shaykh Mohammad b. Ya'qūb, Theqat ol-Islam, *Osūl al-Kāfī*, 1:421; *Kamāl od-Dīn*, in the introduction to the *Masnaf* and 2:475; Mofīd, Shaykh, *al-Ershād*, 2:321.

If we approach the question from the perspective of faith in the Islamic scriptural sources and in the scholarly consensus, we must first determine whether or not the matter of the *act of appointment* to the leadership of the community is one which God reserves for Himself (as the Shī'a believe and have attained to faith in); within this possibility, we see that the Quran gives us an example of such an act of appointment in the prophethood of a child:

$$\text{يَا يَحْيَىٰ خُذِ الْكِتَابَ بِقُوَّةٍ ۖ وَآتَيْنَاهُ الْحُكْمَ صَبِيًّا}$$

> [19:12] [And when the son was born and grew to be a child, came the command,] "O John (*Yaḥyā*)! Hold fast unto the divine writ with [all thy] strength!" – for We granted him wisdom [to judge between men] while he was yet a little boy.

However, if we consider that the act of appointment to the leadership of the community has been delegated by God to the Muslims themselves, and that therefore this act, like all other acts of the community of those who have attained to faith falls within the jurisdiction and guidelines of the sacred law (i.e. is *tashrī'ī*), then the objection might arise that the child in question falls in the category of those who are legally incompetent (*maḥjūrīn*; on account of the fact that he has not yet reached maturity and therefore has not reached the age of legal majority), and so has no sovereignty (*welāya'*) over himself, and is *himself* in need of a guardian (*qayyem*); and so in this case the question would arise: How can one who does not have sovereignty over himself have sovereignty over others?

So we see that the community of Muslims differ on this question: the four-fold legal rites[170] of the Sunnīs all believe the matter of the succession (caliphate) and the imāmate (religio-legal leadership) and sovereignty over the community (*welāya'*) to be an issue which has been delegated by God ﷻ to the Muslims themselves, and that it falls within the aegis of the acts of man (which are governed by the sacred law; i.e. is *tashrī'ī*), and do not consider it to be an act which God ﷻ reserves for Himself. Whereas in the rite of the *Ahl al-Bayt* or in the beliefs of the Shī'a, the act of appointment to the leadership of the community is believed to be a divine prerogative and an act of God, and the matter of attaining to faith in this belief is considered so important that it is considered to be one of the five first principles or creedal principles of the faith.[171]

It is on the basis of this basic belief that the followers of the *Ahl al-Bayt* (the Members of the Household of the Prophet ﷺ) believe in the imāmate of a number of the *Ahl al-Bayt* during their childhood, including Imām Mahdī ﷻ. This belief is in harmony with their creedal beliefs, and no objection can legitimately be raised against it while the Quran continues to be

---

[170] Mālekī, Hanafī, Shāfe'ī and Hanbalī.
[171] *Towhīd*, *Nobowwa'* and *Ma'ād* (which we share with our Sunnī brothers in faith), and the Imāmate (*Imāma'*) and *'Adl* (God's justness), which are the two additional principles which the Shī'a add.

the touchstone of the community and continues to stipulate the prophethood of John ﷺ while he was yet a child.

Nor can any valid objections be raised against this belief from the point of view of the sacred law. From the point of view of the Shī'a this issue (the act of appointment of the leader of the community) does not fall within the aegis of the acts of man (which are governed by the sacred law; i.e. the act is not *tashrī'ī*), but rather, falls within the ambit of creedal beliefs to which faith must be attained. The ordinances within the sacred law which govern guardianship (*welāya*) over the category of legally incompetent persons (*mahjūrīn*) applies to the obligors[172] (*mokallefīn*; those who owe a religious obligation [to God]), and does not apply to God ﷻ the Sublimely Exalted, as it is, He Who determined these ordinances in the first place and made them binding upon man.

---

[172] This word is borrowed from the coffers of the legal profession, wherein it is defined as follows: "the person or entity who owes an obligation to another, as one who must pay on a promissory note." It is being used for the Arabic word *mokallaf*, which is the passive participle of *taklīf*, which in turn is a duty owed to God ﷻ by Moslems as per the requirements of His revealed law, the *sharī'a'*. In his 1941 landmark translation of Shaykh as-Saduq's *A Shi'ite Creed*, the late great A. A. A. Fayzee states: "*Taklīf is* so used [such] that God ﷻ is *mokallef* (one who applies or enforces *taklīf*), while man is *mokallaf* (one to whom *taklīf* is applied or upon whom it is enforced). In English we would say: God ﷻ sets up and enforces the rule of law while man is obliged to obey it."

Thus, one of the reasons for the stipulation of the prophethood of John while he was still a child was for the express purpose of elucidating the point that the imāmate, just like prophethood, is a divine function; and as such, it is not subject to any human criteria or even to criteria which are given to man in the divine canon revealed by God ﷻ with which man is to order his affairs. So the fact of the prophethood of John ﷺ while he was still a child teaches us that attaining to belief in matters of faith are based on reason and [on the proffering of rational and/ or scriptural] proofs, such that if a reason is provided [by God, by way of scripture,] which establishes the imāmate of a minor, one must submit to it and accept it, just as we accept the prophethood of a minor based on Quranic evidence. Given this, it is not appropriate for some to then make excuses by saying things like 'What does the prophethood of the prophet John ﷺ have to do with the imāmate of Imām Mahdī ﷻ? – simply because the prophethood of the prophet John ﷺ has been mentioned explicitly in the Quran whereas this is not the case with the imāmate of Imām Mahdī ﷻ.

This point shows that the objections of Eben Hajar al-Heythamī and the like are without any foundation. He writes in a tone that is not appropriate to learned scholarship as follows: "It has been ordained in the pure sacred law of Islam that minors cannot have sovereignty (*welāyaʿ*) [over the community of Muslims]; given this, how then can a bunch of inattentive fools have accepted the sovereignty of an individual who is only five years of age...?"[173] When we examine the historical evidence, we see that Imām Mahdī ﷻ takes on the burden of the imāmate after the death of his father, meaning that he has indeed been endowed with the spiritual, intellectual, and physical attributes to take on this heavy burden of responsibility during his childhood. Shahīd Sadr writes in this regard:

> The issue of the imāmate [being vested in an Imām] before [he reaches] the age of majority is one that has a precedent in some of the honorable forefathers of His Eminence [the Imām al-Mahdī ﷻ]. Imām Jawād ؏ took on the responsibility of the imāmate when he was eight,[174] and Imām Hādī ؏ did so when he was nine,[175] and Imām Hasan al-Askarī ؏ was vested with the imāmate when twenty-two years had passed of his noble life. As can be seen, the issue of the imāmate being vested in an Imām during his childhood has had antecedents in the lifetimes of some of the other Imāms, and it is a phenomenon which had to some extent become a norm and had been given the seal of acceptance by the public,

---

[173] Eben Hajar, *as-Sawā'eq ol-Mahraqa*, p. 256.

[174] Eben Sabbāq al-Mālekī, *al-Fosūl al-Mohemma*, p. 253; Mofīd, Shaykh, *al-Ershād*, 2:274.

[175] Eben Hajar, *as-Sawā'eq ol-Mahraqa*, p. 312 – 313; See also, Āmelī, Seyyed Tāj ed-Dīn, *at-Tatamma fī Tawārīkh ol-Aemma*.

and this in itself is the best evidence for [the acceptability of] this phenomenon.[176]

At this point, we would like to draw the readers' attention to the following points:

1. The imāmate is not the same as hereditary kingships such as was the case with the Fātemid or Abbāsid caliphates; rather, the Imām must be endowed with special spiritual and intellectual attributes for him to be able to lead the Islamic community in the right spiritual and ideological direction.

2. The cornerstones of these norms were laid at the time of the advent of Islam, and their foundations were fortified and developed during the imāmates of Imām Bāqer ﷺ and Imām Sādeq ﷺ, during whose tenures a great intellectual current was founded and directed, such that hundreds of magisters (*faqīhs*; the theologians cum doctors of sacred law) and *motekallemīn* (masters of the science of *kalām*: creedal or dogmatic theology) and Quranic exegetes and scholars expert in the Quranic

---

[176] 47 Eben Hajar, *as-Sawā'eq ol-Mahraqa*, p. 312-13; Mofīd, Shaykh, *al-Ershād*, 2:281. Both these authorities have related the debate between Imām Jawād ﷺ and Yahyā b. Aktham which took place in the reign of the Abbāsid caliph al-Ma'mūn; and it must be asked how the Imām who was a child at the time was able to defeat Yahyā b. Aktham with all of his intellectual powers and scholarly prowess?

sciences were trained and delivered to the Islamic community under their auspices. Hasan b. Ali al-Washā states, "I entered the [congregational] mosque at Kūfa, and I saw nine hundred shaykhs, all of whom would say, 'Ja'far b. Mohammad has related to us that ...'"[177]

3. The conditions which the Imāms of the School of the *Ahl al-Bayt* have determined which an Imām must have are extremely stringent, under which not just anybody can qualify; one of these conditions is that he must be the most learned person of his time.[178]

4. The followers of the *Ahl al-Bayt* (the Members of the Household of the Prophet) suffered much personal and financial injury because of their beliefs because the ruling powers considered them to be their enemies, at

---

[177] Āmeli, Seyyed Amīn, *al-Majāles as-Sunniya*, 2:468. This event is so famous that both Sunni and Shī'a historians of *hadīth* have related it. For more information, refer to the *Sehāh ol-Akhbār* of Mohammad Serāj od-Dīn ar-Refāhī, page 44; as well as to Asad Heydar's *al-Imām as-Sādeq wa al-Madhāheb ol-Arba'a*, 1:55; and Eben Hajar, *as-Sawā'eq ol-Mahraqa*, p. 305.

[178] Being the most learned person of the era is one of the givens of the criteria of leadership within Shī'a Islam, as Allāme Hellī has stated on page 44 of his *al-Bāb al-Hādī Ashar*. The Imāms were constantly being challenged about this matter and would always pass these tests honorably. Eben Hajar has described in detail a debate which has taken place between Imām Jawād and Yahyā b. Aktham in his *as-Sawāeq ol-Mahraqa* (page 312).

least ideologically. Thus, they put some to death and threw countless others into their dungeons, in which many lost their lives. Therefore, the followers of the *Ahl al-Bayt* ﷺ have always paid a high price for the maintenance of their beliefs;[179] but because they believed in the righteousness of their beliefs, they stood by them and would welcome torture and martyrdom with open arms.

5. The Imāms of the Shī'a, who were endowed with special attributes, lived side by side with the people and would not withdraw themselves from their midst unless the ruling powers exiled or imprisoned them or cut off their relations with their followers in some other way. This we know from the thousands of *hadīth* reports which scholars and ordinary people have reported concerning the Imāms, as well as from the record of their correspondence. The Imāms also established and maintained relationships with people as a consequence of their journeys and by sending envoys and representatives to various places; they had also recommended to their followers to stop by Medina[180] after having made their Hajj pilgrimage so that they could meet their Imām and put questions to him. All of these are indications of the

---

[179] Cf. Esfahānī, Abī'l-Faraj, *Maqātel ot-Tābeīn*, where the author relates some examples of these hardships.

[180] See, for example, Koleynī, Shaykh Mohammad b. Ya'qūb, *Osūl al-Kāfī*, 1:329.

deep bond which existed between the Imāms and their Shī'a (followers).

6. The ruling powers considered the spiritual leadership of the Imāms as a danger which confronted them. They therefore strove to damage this leadership and to destroy it by any possible means, and at times displayed an extraordinary bloodlust and barbarism in effecting this goal,[181] despite the abhorrence of the Muslim masses of their atrocious and repulsive behavior.

Taking the above points into consideration, there can be no doubt that the imāmate during childhood was something that really took place, because one of the most important attributes of the Imām is that he be preeminent in knowledge and wisdom. If this was not the case, the ruling powers could easily arrange public debates and invite the great scholars of the time who were followers of the caliphs to debate and thereby to shame the Imāms. This would preclude the need for any physical coercion, which would at times cause the Imāms to grow even more in popularity; but history tells us that they avoided this method, which would otherwise have been easier and a preferred method, if it were not for the fact of the Imāms' preeminence in knowledge.

---

[181] See, for example, Eben Sabbāq al-Mālekī, *al-Fosūl al-Mohemma*; Esfahānī, Abī'l-Faraj, *Maqātel ot-Tābeīn*; and Mofīd, Shaykh, *al-Ershād*.

Thus, the only reason for the silence of the ruling powers in the face of the superiority of knowledge of the Imāms even during the tenure of those who were vested with the imāmate in their childhood was their certainty in their preeminence and superiority of knowledge. This is why they resorted to the power of the bludgeon and the sword, by means of which they were intent on destroying the Imāms and their followers, and they resorted to formal debates with them very rarely. This is a clear demonstration of the appointed nature of the imāmate, which God ﷻ bestows on whomsoever He wills; for a child, no matter how intelligent – even if he is at the level of a genius – cannot debate the great scholars of a world empire and put them to shame. The office of the imāmate, when it is vested to an Imām in his childhood, is similar to the office of prophethood which was vested on the prophet John ؑ, as God ﷻ the Sublimely Exalted has stated in the Quran:

$$\text{يَا يَحْيَىٰ خُذِ الْكِتَابَ بِقُوَّةٍ ۖ وَآتَيْنَاهُ الْحُكْمَ صَبِيًّا}$$

[19:12] [And when the son was born and grew to be a child, came the command,] "O John (*Yahyā*)! Hold fast unto the divine writ with [all thy] strength!" – for We granted him wisdom [to judge between men] while he was yet a little boy.

When it has been proven that these offices have been vested on leaders prior to their having reached the age of legal majority, there can be no grounds for objecting to the vesting of the imāmate on Imām Mahdī ﷺ during his childhood.[182]

3. The Occultation and Long Life of the Mahdī

From the vantage of the *Ahl al-Bayt* ﷺ, one of the requirements and specific attributes of the Mahdī ﷺ is that he disappear from view until such a time that God ﷻ gives him permission to reappear. The extended lifespan of the Imām should be considered under the following two headings:

3.1 Proof of the possibility of long lifespans

Shahīd Sayyed Mohammad Bāqer as-Sadr asks in this regard:

Is it possible for an individual to have a life whose duration spans centuries, as is claimed about the lifespan of Imām Mahdī ﷺ, whose age is now believed to extend to over a thousand years? Here the word "possible" can have three possible meanings:

1. Possibility in practice or the question as to whether something is practically possible.
2. Possibility according to scientific considerations or the question as to whether something is scientifically possible.
3. Logical or philosophical possibility.

---

[182] Shahīd Mohammad Bāqer as-Sadr, *Bahth Howl al-Mahdī*, pages 93 to 99.

What is meant by whether something is "practically possible" is whether it is a feat that is possible in practice, such as going to the moon or to the depths of the oceans.

What is meant by whether something is "scientifically possible" is that in the present world, given present capabilities, certain things are not (yet) possible, such as going to the planet Mars, but at the same time, there are no theoretical restrictions on such a feat, and that science could in time bring it into the realm of possibility. However, science will never make it possible to go to the Sun, because science considers it to be beyond the realm of possibility to devise an instrument that can withstand millions of degrees of temperature.

And finally, what is meant by whether something is "logically or philosophically possible" is the rules that the intellect holds which precludes the exclusion of the reality of anything prior to the examination of any experiential data, and which places such data in the category of the possible. For example, the intellect considers the division of three [whole] oranges into two equal parts without halving one to be a logical impossibility because three is an odd number and it is not logically possible to divide an odd number by an even whole integer. But it is logically possible for one to enter a fire and not to burn, because it is possible for there not to be a heat transfer from the hotter (burning) body to the cooler one.

Thus, we can conclude that the ambit or compass of "logical possibility" is wider than that of "scientific possibility", and that the ambit of "scientific possibility" is wider than that of "practical possibility." And there is no doubt that the extension of a human life beyond its normal limits is logically possible, as imagining the occurrence of such a hypothetical event is certainly not impossible, and there is no logical obstacle which prevents one from imagining such a hypothetical possibility, because life is not necessarily concomitant with a quick death.

Similarly, there is no doubt that long lifespans are not possible in practice, because we do not as yet have all of the scientific means to bring about long life, and mankind has not been able to experience extended life-durations which span many centuries in the present age, but this is certainly possible from the vantage of science, which is why researchers are working every day on discovering the key to longevity so that they can extend the human lifespan. In effect, old age is the weakening and decay of cells and tissue and organs as a result of contact with external elements, all of which can, in theory, be delayed for extended periods.

Thus, greatly extended lifespans are possible both logically and scientifically, even though they are not a practical possibility yet. However, it is possible that long lifespans will also be practically possible at some point in the future. Thus, it should not be strange that Imām Mahdī ﷻ should have an extended lifespan, because it is possible that he has been given access to certain sciences and possibilities which have so far remained hidden from ordinary mortals. For example, the Most Noble

Prophet ﷺ was able to journey in one night from the Masjed al-Harām (the Sacred Sanctuary; the Ka'ba) to the Masjed al-Aqsa (the Farthest Sanctuary or the al-Aqsa Mosque in Jerusalem), and this feat was made practically possible for him by the grace of God ﷻ. This is also possible now, after the passage of fourteen hundred years, for human beings to travel this distance in an hour by airplane. The Almighty God ﷻ has similarly made an extended lifespan practically possible for Imām Mahdī ﷻ; and it is likewise possible for mankind someday to master the science necessary to extend lifespans.

What is interesting to note is that some people accept the possibility of the extended lifespan of the prophet Noah ؑ which is mentioned in the Quran, but are unwilling to accept even the possibility of the extended lifespan of Imām Mahdī ﷻ. To these people we pose the question: Do you not have faith in the Quran and in the prophetic *hadīth* corpus, that you deny the *possibility* of extended lifespans in others? There are also other examples of breaches in the normal laws of nature in the Quran, such as the failure of fire to burn the great prophet Abraham ؑ, or the parting of the waters of the Red Sea in order to give passage to the great prophet Moses ؑ and his people, and so on. Thus, it is clear not only that an extended lifespan is within the realms of logical and scientific possibility for Imām Mahdī ﷻ, but that it is also in the realm of practical possibility, with God's leave.

3.2 Proof of the Longevity of Imām Mahdī's Life
We shall approach the discussion here under the two headings of creedal belief and historical evidence.

3.2.1 The approach from the vantage of creedal belief
This topic can be presented in three ways:

The First Approach
The extended lifespan of Imām Mahdī ﷻ is one of the innate characteristics of the concept of Mahdism in the beliefs of the School of the *Ahl al-Bayt* ﷺ. This attribute was proven by means of a categorical proof and naturally leads us to believe in the occultation of the Twelfth Imām ﷻ. According to this scriptural proof, if we grant that as long as the Imāms which are to succeed the Prophet ﷺ are to be twelve in number, and as long as we grant that it is a fact that the world will come to an end with the last of the series of these twelve Imāms; and if we also grant – as the Shī'a believe – that all twelve of these Imāms have been appointed to the office of the leadership of the community of Muslims by Almighty God ﷻ and that the people have no say whatsoever in this appointment to that office or removal from that office; then it follows that we must accept that because the other eleven Imāms have already come and gone, the life of the twelfth must necessarily be extended until the end of the world.

Now if it is stated that the life of Imām Mahdī ﷻ has a natural lifespan like those of everyone else, and that he will die after a natural span of life and will re-emerge at the end of time, we respond as follows: if this hypothesis was true, the earth would be bereft of God's *hojjat*[183] and this would be at variance with the meaning of the Hadīth of the Two Weighty Trusts[184] which posits the necessary concomitance of the Quran and the Family (*etra'*) of the Prophet ﷺ until the Day of Resurrection. Additionally, this hypothetical scenario would necessitate belief in the *raj'a* (the coming back to earth of the dead) of Imām Mahdī ﷻ, and this is something that no Muslim believes in and for which there is no scriptural basis.

The Second Approach

The extended lifespan of Imām Mahdī ﷻ is one of the characteristics that has been attributed to him in the Shī'a *hadīth* report corpus, and in some of the Sunnī sources of *hadīth* scripture, such as Qondūzī's *Yanabī al-Mawadda*, in which, quoting the *Farāed al-Moslemīn*, it is related from Imām Bāqer ﷺ, who reports from his father back to his ancestor Alī b. Abī-Tāleb ﷺ who reports the Apostle of God ﷺ to have said,

---

[183] *Hojjat* or *hojjatollāh*: the Proof [of God] [36:12] ... For of all things do We take account in a manifest Imām (*imāmin mobīn*) [who shall be called to testify and provide evidence on all matters on the Day of Judgment]. This is the meaning of the word *hojjatollāh* or God's proof for mankind, which is one of the names given to the Imāms by the Quran: The *hojjat* is the perfect embodiment and "clear evidence" of all truth on Earth and the conclusive argument and evidentiary proof against all falsehood on Judgement Day.

[184] See footnote #162 on page 177.

"Mahdī is one of my offspring who will be occulted (*takūnᵘ lahū ghayba*), and when he appears, he will fill the world with equity and justice after it has become full of iniquity and injustice."[185]

In this same book, it is reported from Saī'd b. Jobayr from Eben Abbās who reports the Apostle of God ﷺ to have said, "Verily Ali ؑ is my *wasī* (inheritor, legatee, executor and successor), and al-Qāem al-Montazer (the Awaited One who will Rise Up [in insurrection against injustice and oppression]) is one of his progeny who will fill the world with equity and justice after it has become full of iniquity and injustice. I swear upon [my oath] to He Who has commissioned me in truth as a giver of glad tidings and as a warner [to all mankind]! Those who remain steadfast [in their loyalty] to his imāmate during [the period of] his occultation are rarer than Red Sulphur!' At this juncture, Jāber arose and asked, 'O Apostle of God ﷺ! Will there be a [period of] occultation for the Qāem (the One who will Rise Up [in insurrection against injustice and oppression]) who is [to be] one of your progenies?' The Apostle of God ﷺ stated, 'Yes, by God! Verily, my Lord of Providence selects at every moment those who have attained to faith [in His Providence] and destroys the unbelievers.' He then said, 'O Jāber! Verily, this is a matter from among the divine decrees and a secret from among the divine secrets, so do not harbor doubts in it, for doubting divine decrees is [tantamount to] unbelief (*kofr*).'"[186]

---

[185] Qondūzī, *Yanabī al-Mawadda*, 3:296 (Chapter 78).
[186] Qondūzī, *Yanabī al-Mawadda*, 3:297 (Chapter 78).

On the same page, it is reported from Hasan b. Khāled that His Eminence Imām Ali b. Mūsā ar-Redā ﷺ has stated, "The fourth [generation] of my progeny who is born to the Lady of the Bondsmaidens [of Heaven] will be born and God ﷻ will cleanse the earth from all tyranny and oppression [by means of his leadership], and he is a person in whose birth people will have doubts, and he will have a prolonged occultation, after which he will appear and fill the earth with the light of his Lord of Providence (*bi nūr^u rabbohā*)"[187]

In this same book it is related from Ahmad b. Zīad, who reports from Do'abl b. Ali al-Khazāī: "I entered into [the presence of] Imām Redā ﷺ and recited the Tāīya ode, at which point Imām Redā ﷺ said, 'The Imāms after me shall be Mohammad b. Ali ﷺ, Ali b. Mohammad ﷺ, Hasan b. Ali ﷺ and after him will be his son, the Hojja^t and the Qāem ﷺ. He will be in [a state of] occultation and will await his [re]appearance, after which he will be obeyed and God ﷻ will fill the world with justice and equity by means of him, after it will have become filled with injustice and oppression. But as to when he will appear, my father has related from his forefathers before him from the Apostle of God ﷺ that his advent is like the advent of the Day of Resurrection which will appear suddenly."[188]

---

[187] *Ibid.*
[188] *Ibid.*

In this book, it is reported by Ghāyaṭ b. al-Marām, from Farāed os-Samtayn, from Jāber b. Abdollāh in the form of an "elevated" or *marfū'*[189] *hadīth* report that the Prophet said,

> "The Mahdī ﷻ is of my progeny and will have the same name and honorific (*konya*) as me. He will have the greatest likeness to me of all people in terms of his physical appearance as well as his character. He will have a period where he will be occulted from view, in which time nations will be led astray, and he will appear suddenly like a comet and will fill the world with justice and equity after it will have become filled with injustice and oppression."

Also, it is reported again in *Farāed os-Samtayn*, from Imām Bāqer ؑ from his forefathers back to Imām Alī b. Abī-Tāleb ؑ, who has related [that the Prophet ﷺ said]: "The Mahdī ﷻ is of

---

[189] A *marfū' hadīth* is a particular type of *morsal hadīth* in which one or more transmitters are missing from the middle or tail end of its *sanad* or provenance title (the chain of transmitters that appear in the report before the actual text which determines the integrity or lack thereof of the report's chain of custody), and in which the word *rafa'a* appears, as in the sentence, 'Shaykh Koleynī heard reported from Alī b. Ebrāhīm and "*rafa'a an*" Imam as-Sādeq. In other words, what we would say in English "[and so on] *up to* the Imām." This sort of "elevation" without reference to the names of the transmitters that are supposed to make up the rungs of the ladder that go "up" to the original source is a sure sign of a *morsal hadīth* report.

my progeny and will have a period where he will be occulted [from view] during which time nations will become bewildered and will be led astray... and he will fill the world with justice and equity after it will have become filled with injustice and oppression."

And again in the same book, it is reported from Manāqeb from Imām Bāqer ؏ ... who has related that the Prophet ﷺ said: "Happy the soul who is present when the Qāem of my Household appears and who has chosen him as his Imām during the period of his occultation and before his advent, and who is a friend to those who befriend him and an enemy to those who have enmity toward him. Such a person is a friend of mine and shall be the best of people from within my nation on the Day of Resurrection."

And again in the same book, it is reported from Abū-Basīr from Imām Sādeq ؏ from his forefathers back to Imām Alī b. Abī-Tāleb ؏, who has related that the Prophet ﷺ said: "The Mahdī ؏ is of my progeny and will have the same name and honorific (*konya*) as me. He will have the greatest likeness to me of all people in terms of his physical appearance as well as his character. There will be a period where he will be occulted from view, in which time people will be led astray from their religions, and at that time, he will appear suddenly like a comet and will fill the world with justice and equity after it will have become filled with injustice and oppression."

In this book, a *hadīth* report that is similar to this one is recorded with the difference that it ends as follows: "...he will appear suddenly like a comet and will bring with him the heritage (*mīrāth*) of the prophets."[190]

On page 494 of Qondūzī's *Yanābī' ol-Mowadda*, it is related from Jāber b. Yazīd aj-Ja'fī: "I heard Jāber b. Abdollāh al-Ansārī say that the Prophet of God told him, 'O Jāber! My successors and the Imāms of the Muslims after me are the following: The first of them is Ali, then Hasan b. Ali, then Hosayn b. Ali, then Ali b. Hosayn and Mohammad b. Ali, whom you will see; give him my greetings of peace! Then Ja'far b. Mohammad, Mūsā b. Ja'far, Ali b. Mūaā, Mohammad b. Ali, Ali b. Mohammad, Hasan b. Ali, and then the Qāem, who will have the same name and honorific (*konya*) as me. He is the son of Hasan b. Ali through whom [God] will conquer the East and the West through him. He is the same person who will enter into [a period of] occultation and will disappear from the view of the *owlīā*[191] and no one will be steadfast [in their allegiance] to his imāmate except those whose hearts have been tested for faith by God."

---

[190] Qondūzī, *Yanābī' ol-Mowadda*, 3:397.

[191] Those of God's creatures who have spiritual proximity to Him; singular, *walīy*, inclusive of prophets and Imāms and, to a lesser degree, the *olamā* and *foqahā*.

The Third Approach

If the Promised Mahdī ﷻ was not an Immaculate[192] Imām but was an ordinary person like every other Muslim, in this case there would be no similarities between him and the prophet Jesus ؏; whereas Jesus ؏ is one of the five *olu'l-azm* apostles (great prophets; literally meaning 'those endowed with [a great] resolve') who will endorse the Mahdī's leadership and call upon the Christians to follow the Mahdī in Islam. Therefore, the Mahdī ﷻ must necessarily be immaculate (*ma'sūm*).

Furthermore, being immaculate is not a matter of personal choice or something that one can claim for oneself but is something that must be bestowed upon one by God ﷻ. This appointment and divine investiture to succession are effected by the categorical scriptural imperatives of the Prophet ﷺ (*nusūs*) – imperatives which do not obtain in any *hadīth* reports in favor of anyone other than the Twelve Imāms of the Most Noble Prophet's ﷺ Purified Household, even at the level of a claim to such investiture, let alone the possibility of a historical fact that is supported by empirical, rational and scriptural proofs (as is the case with the investiture of the Twelve Imāms).

Additionally, it was established earlier that eleven of the twelve Imāms had died and that their bodies have been buried in publicly known locations, and that it is only the Twelfth Imām

---

[192] Inerrant as well as sinless, in accordance with how the Shī'a define the concept.

ﷻ who remains and whose death has not been announced or proven. Therefore, we must believe in the extension of his life from the time of his birth to the end of time; and it is only this person who is worthy of being affirmed by the prophet Jesus ؑ and to be worthy of being his Imām.

Sayyed Sāmī al-Badrī writes: "The way in which the Sunnīs conceive of the Mahdī is such that he would never be able [to command] leadership over Jesus ؑ, and he would not even be able to gather the various sects of the Muslims around himself and to lead them [as a unified nation]. [In this conception,] he is not capable of leading Jesus ؑ because Jesus ؑ is an apostle sent by God ﷻ who is immaculate and has miracles to prove the divine origins of his mission, and it is not possible for a person to have leadership over him whose legitimacy and credentials are not affirmed by his having been endowed with miracles and immaculacy and perfect knowledge, and such a person will never be able to unite all of the Muslims under his banner without such miracles and immaculacy and perfect knowledge."[193]

3.2.2 The approach from the vantage of historical evidence
This topic can also be presented in three ways:

The First Approach
History testifies to the birth of Imām Mahdī ﷻ and news of his death has not been recorded in the annals of history. This

---

[193] 63 al-Badrī, Seyyed Sāmī, *ash-Shobahāt al-Wardūd*, Book 4, page 32.

suffices to let us know that his life has continued, and in so far as we do not know of anyone other than the son of Imām Hasan al-Askarī ؑ to be identified as the Mahdī, then it follows that his continued life must be one which is veiled from the eyes of people.

The Second Approach

History testifies to the fact that during the era of the occultation, there have been repeated cases of eye witnesses having seen Imām Mahdī ﷻ, and as was discussed earlier, there are books that have been written on this specific subject, such as Sayyed Hāshem al-Bahrānī's *Tabsera' al-Walī fī man Ra'y al-Qāem al-Mahdī*.

Shaykh Abū-Tāleb at-Tajlīl at-Tabarī has gathered the names of 266 people who have testified to seeing Imām Mahdī ﷻ during the lesser occultation, citing most of their reports.[194] He has devoted a separate chapter to those who have seen Imām Mahdī ﷻ during the greater occultation, and cites twenty books which are compilations of *hadīth* reports related by people who tell the tale of their meeting with the Imām.

We shall relate one such story here, which makes its appearance in Sayyed Sadreddīn as-Sadr's *al-Mahdī*, where Sadr quotes Shaykh Abdol-Wahhāb ash-She'rānī in the book *Tabaqāt ol-Orafā* (Stations of the Mystics), which is an intellectual biography of Shaykh Hasan Erāqī.

---

[194] at-Tabarī, Shaykh Abū-Tāleb at-Tajlīl, *Man Hūa al-Mahdī?*

"I went to see him together with Abol-Abbās Harīthī. He said, 'Will you allow me to relate my story from its beginning up to the present day, such that [you would be informed of my life story to such an extent that] one would say you were my friend and companion from childhood?'

I said, 'Yes.'

He said, 'In my youth, I was a Damascene youth who worked in a workshop. We gathered around with the other youth [of the neighborhood] on Fridays, and would have fun and play games and drink wine. One day I came to myself and thought, "Is this [frivolity] the purpose for which I was created?"'

I quit that circle of frivolity and escaped their clutches. They came after me but did not find me. I went to the Banī-Omayya congregational mosque. There I saw that there was a preacher seated at the pulpit (*manbar*) talking about the Mahdī ﷻ. I became eager to see him, to the point that there was not a single prostration of mine in which I did not ask God ﷻ the Sublimely Exalted to honor me with this privilege.

One night, after the evening devotions (*namāz-e maghreb*), I was engaged in performing the supererogatory devotions when someone sat behind me, laid his hand on my shoulder and said, 'My son, God ﷻ the Sublimely Exalted has responded to your supplications. What is it that you need? I am the Mahdī.'

I said, 'Will you come with me to my house?'

He said, 'Yes.'

He came to my house and said, 'Prepare a quiet spot for me.'

I dedicated a quiet spot to him, and he stayed with me for seven days and nights, after which he left."[195]

Shaykh Ali b. Īsā al-Arbalī writes in *Kashf ol-Ghamma*: "People relate stories and tales which contain extraordinary events and occurrences concerning their meetings with Imām Mahdī ﷻ, the retelling of which would take a lot of time; I [therefore] have selected two such tales which are chronologically close to our own time, both of which have been related to me by a group of reliable brothers [in faith]."

The First Tale

There was a man by the name of Ismāīl who lived in the town of Hella, which is situated between the Tigris and the Euphrates. My brothers told me that Ismāīl related his tale as follows:

"A tumor the size of a fist had formed on my left thigh, and the physicians of Hella were at a loss as to how to cure the condition. I journeyed to Baghdad and went to see Western (*farangī*; literally, Frankish) doctors. These all told me that there is no cure

---

[195] As-Sadr, Seyyed Sadroddīn, *al-Mahdī*, p. 149.

for my condition. I then went on a pilgrimage to Sāmarrā[196] to pay my respects to the Imāms al-Hādī ﷺ and Hasan al-Askarī ﷺ. I also went to the Sacred Cellar[197] and made my supplications there. Then I went to the Tigris, washed my clothes and put them on. At this point, I saw four horsemen leaving the gates of the city. One of them was an old man who held a spear in his hand, and there was a young man who wore colorful clothes. The old man who held a spear in his hand was on the right side of the path, and two young men were on the left, and the young man who wore colorful clothes was in the middle.

He asked me, 'Will you be going back to your family tomorrow?'

I said, 'Yes.'

He said, 'Come closer so that I can see what ails you.'

---

[196] About 125 km north of Baghdad.

[197] The cellar of the residence of Imām Hasan al-Askarī ﷺ which is presently located in the northwest corner of the shrine of the Askarīayn (Imām Hādī ﷺ and Imām Hasan al-Askarī ﷺ), where it is said both Imāms performed their devotions during the hot days of summer. According to some reports, Imām Mahdī ﷺ has been seen in this cellar, both before and after his occultation, which is why it is sometimes referred to as the Cellar of the Occultation. Some Sunnis maintain that the Shī'a believe that the Mahdī ﷺ was secreted away in a cellar after his birth and started his occultation from there and is still living in that cellar, out of which he will arise at the time of his advent, but there is no textual evidence for such a belief in the Shī'a sources.

I went forward. He put his hand on my tumor and squeezed it, which caused me a lot of pain. He then straddled his mount. The old man with the spear in his hand said, 'You have prospered, O Ismāīl! This man is your Imām!'

They started off, and I started to follow them, but the Imām said, 'Head back!'

I said, 'I will never part your company!'

The Imām said, 'That which is expedient is that you should head back.'

I said, 'No. I will never leave your side!'

The old man said, 'O Ismāīl! Have you no shame? The Imām has told you twice to head back, and you object?!'

I stopped. The Imām took a few steps toward me and said, 'O Ismāīl! When you reach Baghdad, Abū-Ja'far [= the Abbāsid caliph al-Mostansar bi'llāh] will summon you. If you go to him and he gives you something, do not accept it from him; and tell our son ar-Reda to write a letter to Ali b. 'Awd, and I will instruct him to give you whatever you desire [in compensation].'

The party then left and I stood still and looked at them until they disappeared from view. Then I sat in a corner for a while weeping with sadness, then I went [back] to Sāmarrā. There a throng gathered around me, asking, 'What happened? Why have you lost color?'

I said, 'Did you recognize those riders who left the city gate for the bank of the river?'

They said, 'They were of the nobility, and are among the great herdsmen.'

I said, 'Rather, they were the Lord of the Age ﷻ and his companions!' The young man who wore colorful clothing was the Imām who placed his hand on my wound and healed it.'

They said, 'Show us the wound!'

I showed them the place of the tumor and they saw that it had healed and that there was no trace of any wound. They threw themselves on me and ripped my clothes to shreds for they considered them to have been consecrated [to have healing properties and be charged with blessings...], and they took me home so that the throng [that had gathered around me] would disperse. Afterwards, the caliph's deputy of the Treasury came and asked me about my name, parentage, address, the date I left Baghdad and about some other thing, and then left.

I spent that night in the Treasury, and left the town with some other folk after performing the morning devotions. They escorted me for a portion of the way and then returned. I travelled alone for a while until I reached a place where some people were gathered. When they saw me and got to know my name and parentage, they took off my clothes and cut them into pieces and kept them as consecrated relics (i.e. for their *tabarrok*[198] value].

The caliph's representative had informed the court and the caliph of what had happened by letter. The vizier Sa'īd had summoned Radīoddīn in order to ascertain the veracity of the news. He [Radīoddīn] was a friend of mine and was my host prior to my departure for Sāmarrā. When Radīoddīn and his associates saw me, I dismounted and showed them the spot where the tumor used to be. Radīoddīn fainted for a short spell, then took my hand and while tears were running down his cheeks, we entered the presence of the vizier and [he] said, 'This is my brother and the person who is closest to me.'

The vizier asked about what had happened and ordered the physicians whom I had consulted [prior to this incident] to be summoned. They were asked about the date on which they had been consulted and they said, 'Ten days ago.'

The vizier showed them the place of the wound where no trace of a large tumor could be seen. The foreign doctors said, 'This is a miracle of Jesus ﷺ.'

The vizier said, 'Rather, we know better to whom this miracle belongs.' The vizier then took me to the caliph, and the caliph

---

[198] The property of a relic or some mundane object which has been blessed or charged in some other way with sacral properties.

asked about the incident. I explained everything to him, and he ordered that I be given a thousand Dinārs.[199]

I said, "I cannot accept a single one of those coins.'

The caliph asked, 'Fear of whom prevents you from accepting this?'

I said, 'The person who cured me told me not to accept anything from Abū-Ja'far.' And when the caliph heard this, he began to weep.

Ali b. Īsā says, 'I was in the midst of relating this tale to a crowd of people when I realized one of Ismāīl's sons by the name of Shamseddīn whom I did not know was among them. He [identified himself and] said, 'I am one of his sons.' I asked, 'Did you ever see the wound on your father's thigh?'

He replied, 'I was very little when he had that tumor, but I heard about it from my father, mother, kindred and neighbors; and I have seen the wound of the tumor which had grown over with hair.' He added, 'I told Sayyed Safieddīn Mohammad and Najmeddīn Heydar b. Aysar, 'You who have been witness to Ismāīl's [state both] before and after his cure, relate its tale to me; and his son told me that his father returned to Sāmarrā forty times after his cure in the hope of seeing the Imām again, but without success.

---

[199] Gold coins.

The Second Tale
Sayyed Bāqī b. Atwaᵗ al-Alawī al-Hosaynī related to me:

"His father Atwa did not believe that the Mahdī ﷺ existed. He would say, 'If the Imām comes and cures me of my illness, I will affirm that which the Shī'a believe.' He would constantly repeat this refrain until one day we had gathered to make the night (*eshā*) devotions when my father cried out. We rushed to him, and he said, 'Seek out the Imām, for he just now left my presence. We went out [to look], but did not see anyone. We returned to him and he said, 'Someone came to me and said, "O Atwa!" I said, "Yes?" He said, "I am the Mahdī and I have come to cure you." He then placed his blessed hand on my thigh and squeezed and cured my leg, which has now become spry and nimble!'

Ali b. Īsā says, 'I asked about this matter from people other than his son. All of them affirmed its truth.'"[200]

These reports and others like them are the reasons why some of the great Sunnī scholars avow the reality of the Imām; or that is what is implicit in the words of some of them.

Sayyed Sadreddīn as-Sadr has pointed to some of these scholars and states, "One such person is Mohīeddīn Eben Arabī [who makes his avowal] in *The Meccan Openings* (according to Shaykh Abdol-Wahhāb She'rānī in his *al-Yawāqīb wa'l-Jawāher* which is

---
[200] Qondūzī, *Yanabī al-Mawadda*, 3:315-317.

quoted in *As'āf ar-Rāqebīn*). He says, 'After the death of Imām Hasan al-Askarī in the year 260 Lunar, his son immediately became his successor. And this necessitated the continued existence of Imām Mahdī until his advent, or that he should die and that God should bring him back to life at the time of his reappearance.' [Sayyed Sadreddīn as-Sadr adds:] And it is not thought that Shaykh Mohīeddīn Eben Arabī holds to this latter position."

Also, according to what appears in his *al-Yawāqīb wa'l-Jawāher*, as quoted in *As'āf ar-Rāqebīn*, Shaykh Abdol-Wahhāb She'rānī maintains that, "Mahdī b. al-Hasan al-Askarī was born in the middle of the month of Sha'bān in the year 255 Lunar. He will remain alive until Jesus the son of Mary joins him. This has been related to me by Shaykh Hasan an-Narāqī from Imām Mahdī [himself] when he had been given the honor to be present in his company; and my master Ali al-Khawās agreed with him and affirmed what he said."[201]

Also among the scholars who avow the reality of the extended life of the Imām is Shaykh Abū-Abdollāh Mohammad b. Yūsof b. Mohammad Ganjī, whose book *al-Bayān fī Akhbār Sāheb oz-Zamān* is quoted in *As'āf ar-Rāqebīn*: "Among the reasons that support [the belief in] the long life of the Imām or at a minimum provide for its possibility is the longevity of the life of the prophet Jesus the son of Mary, and that of His Eminence Khedr

---

[201] *As'āf ar-Rāqebīn*, P. 157.

and the prophet Elija ﷺ. The longevity of the lives of the one-eyed Dajjāl and of Satan the Accursed who are both enemies of God ﷻ and whose longevity has been abundantly proven in scripture also provide additional evidence for this possibility. [202]

Another example in this line of reasoning can be seen in the book *Fasl ol-Khetāb* of the learned and wise shaykh, Khāja Mohammad Parsā as quoted by Qondūzī in his *Yanābī' ol-Mowadda*. After mentioning the birth of Imām Mahdī ﷻ, Parsā goes on to state that "God ﷻ bestowed wisdom upon him when he was yet a child, just as He had done so in the case of Jesus ﷺ and John ﷺ, upon whom wisdom and prophethood were bestowed while they were still children. And God ﷻ the Sublimely Exalted determined that the Mahdī's life would be long, just as he had so determined for His Eminence Khedr ﷺ."[203]

Shaykh Sadreddīn Qūnawī is another case in point. In a will addressed to his students, he states: "Sell my books on medicine, *hekmat* (theosophical wisdom) and philosophy and donate their proceeds as charity to the poor. But as to the books on *tafsīr* (Quranic exegesis), *ahādīth* (*hadīth* report compilations) and *tasawwof* (sufism), keep them and preserve them in the library and repeat the formula *lā ilāha ill'allāh* (there is no deity other

---

[202] *As'āf ar-Rāqebīn*, p. 227.
[203] Qondūzī, *Yanābī' ol-Mowadda*, 3:304 (Chapter 79).

than Allāh) one thousand times every night, and give my greetings of peace to Imām Mahdī."[204]

Another case in point is Shaykh Sa'eddīn Homawī, as quoted by Shaykh Azīz b. Mohammad Nafīsī. During the process of recounting the Twelve Imāms of the Ahl al-Bayt which God has appointed as the successors of the honorable Prophet of Islam, he states, "And the last successor of the Most Noble Prophet who is the twelfth *walī* (regent, sovereign, lord and master; patron, guardian, protector, custodian) of God is the Lord of the Age, the Imām al-Mahdī."[205]

Another example can be seen in the works of Shahāboddīn al-Hendī, known as Malek ol-Olamā (the King of the Scholars of Religion). His book *Hedāyat as-Sa'dā'* is quoted in *ad-Dor ol-Mowsūya* where in the process of recounting the Twelve Imāms of the *Ahl al-Bayt* he states, "The son of Imām Hosayn in the ninth generation [after him] is the Occulted Imām, His Eminence the Imām al-Mahdī. He will go into [a state of] occultation [for a period of time] and will have an extended lifespan, as is the case with the longevity of the life of the prophet Jesus the son of Mary, and that of His Eminence Khedr and the prophet Elija among the righteous, and as is the case with the Dajjāl and the Sāmerī among the heretics."

---

[204] Quoted in Qondūzī, *Yanābī' ol-Mowadda*, 3:340 (Chapter 84).
[205] Quoted in Qondūzī, *Yanābī' ol-Mowadda*, 3:352 (Chapter 87).

Islamic Messianism

And finally we see in Qondūzī's *Yanābī' ol-Mowadda* and in many other books a very large number of scholars, sages and adepts who aver the extended lifespan of Imām Mahdī ﷻ in their writings and poetry, both in Arabic as well as in the Persian language, and who own to his being vested with the faculty of *welāya'* (proximity to God; sovereignty over the community of believers) and being vested in the succession to the Prophet ﷺ and the office of the imāmate (religio-political leadership over the community of the believers), and to his being the intermediary through which God's grace is dispensed.[206]

The Third Approach

The Lesser Occultation[207] bears witness to the fact that Imām Mahdī ﷻ lives amid the people, bearing the following explanation in mind. The sudden occultation of Imām Mahdī ﷻ would have dealt a severe blow to the Shī'a faithful because they were constantly in touch and interacted with their Imāms and so the loss of their Imām would have been felt acutely. And so, the Lesser Occultation occurred as a way of preparing the community for the Greater Occultation. During the Lesser

---

[206] *Al-Mahdī*, pages 146 to 148.

[207] The Imām al-Mahdī ﷺ remained in hiding during the early years of his Imāmate, during which time he communicated with his followers through a series of four deputies (*nā'eb*, pl. *nawwāb*). The period where the Imām was in communication with the community of the faithful came to be known as the Lesser Occultation (257 Lunar/ 869 CE) and lasted about seventy-two years, and during this time, the Shī'a maintained their contact with their Imām by way of the four Deputies.

Occultation, the Four Deputies (*nāyeb*, plural *nawwāb*)[208] would see to the needs of the community and act as intermediaries through which answers to questions of the faithful would be obtained from the Imām. These four deputies were:

5. Othmān b. Sa'īd al-'Amrī (260/ 874 – 875)
6. Mohammad b. Othmān al-'Amrī (d. 304/ 916 – 917)
7. Al-Hosayn b. Rūh an-Nowbakhtī (d. 326/ 937 – 938)
8. Ali b. Mohammad as-Sāmarrī (d. 329/ 940 – 941)

Accounts of the lives of these four deputies appear in *Ketāb al-Ghaybaʿ as-Soghrā* (*The Book of the Lesser Occultation*). Each of these deputies would introduce the next deputy to the Shī'a until Ali b. Mohammad as-Sāmarrī announced that he will be the last special deputy, and that after his passing, the Greater Occultation will commence, during which the general deputyship of the community shall be vested in the fully qualified *faqīhs* or

---

[208] During the interim period of 67 years known as the minor occultation, the august and blessed presence of the Imām communicated with his community through a series of four successive deputies (*nāyeb*, plural *nawwāb*). During this time, as well as prior to it (during the time of the previous Imāms), the Imāms designated specific individuals to act on their behalf in all matters having to do with the community of their faithful followers who were in cities and towns far from Medina or other cities such as Kūfa and Sāmarrā where the Imāms were domiciled.

magisters[209] of sound moral character (*ādel*), who will thereby take on the burden of guidance of the community of the faithful.

Thus, the Lesser Occultation provided the groundwork for familiarizing the faithful with what was to come in the Greater Occultation and their referral to the general deputyship of the magisters (*foqahā*).

Lastly, we can add that it is the majority opinion of the Shī'a magisters that it is indeed possible to see the Imām Mahdī ﷻ *in person* during the era of his occultation, though this is a privilege that he grants very rarely.[210]

---

[209] Scholars of the integral religion of Islam which includes sacred jurisprudence, theology and all of the other Quranic sciences.

[210] As a point of disambiguation or in order to disabuse certain readers from a possible misconception which might arise in their minds at this point, we mention here that there appears in one of the noble *towqī'* (written or oral dispensations of the Imāms, especially the Twelfth Imām ﷻ, the Lord of the Age) of His Eminence (the Lord of the Age), the following quote: "It is not possible to see the Lord of the Age clearly and unmistakably during [the Era of] the Occultation;" (Shahīd Mohammad Bāqer as-Sadr, *Bahth Howl al-Mahdī*, pages 108 to 111.) The explanation of this *towqī'* is that it was an utterance of the Imām al-Mahdī during the period of his *lesser* occultation when many people were laying false claims to having seen him and to being his deputy (*wakīl*), and this statement was made by the Imām to put his followers on notice to be wary of imposter deputies. The *towqī'* also placed conditions on who could be a legitimate deputy and how he was to be

3 The Value of Belief in the Concept of Mahdism in Shīʿa Islam

Worldly beliefs whose origins are human and heavenly beliefs which originate in the Divine must both have human significations. Worldly beliefs arise from the environment and the conditions in which man lives and are indicative of ways in which he strives to make a better life for himself, whereas heavenly beliefs which originate in the Divine are indications of the grace and mercy that God ﷻ shows to those who serve Him and His desire to draw his bondsmen to the shore of salvation.

This is a matter which a believer will attain to faith in and become certain of as a principle of his Islamic faith, whether this human understanding is comprehensive or remains in a perfunctory form.

At times, humans approach the matter of their beliefs from the vantage of reasons, evidence and proofs; and at other times from the vantage of whether or not a given belief or position helps to bring about some of their objectives or helps to resolve some of the issues which they face during their daily lives. No matter how strong a rational basis a belief might be able to claim, if it is neutral or problematic in terms of securing one's material considerations, the belief will remain subject to skepticism and doubt and will not find its place in one's heart.

---

identified. Its applicability does not extend to the period of the Greater Occultation, in which different conditions apply.

Islamic beliefs which have a Divine origin take both factors into consideration and seek to secure man's felicity in this world as well as in the hereafter, as is evidenced by the celebrated *āya*:

$$\text{وَمَا أَرْسَلْنَاكَ إِلَّا رَحْمَةً لِّلْعَالَمِينَ}$$

> [21:107] And [thus, O Mohammad ﷺ,] We have not sent thee but as [an evidence of Our] grace for both worlds.

Through our investigations, we reached the conclusion that the concept of Mahdism (or the belief in the coming of a universal savior) is stronger in terms of the scriptural and rational proofs proffered for it in the Shī'a rite compared with the four Sunnī rites, and that this conception is in greater harmony with the Quranic revelations and the prophetic *hadīth* corpus. However, despite this, uncertainties and doubts persist in the minds of certain people, and this is because they do not approach the issue from the vantage of the rational and scriptural evidence that is before them, but rather give priority to worldly interests and considerations.

The minds of these types of people is always posing the question as to what possible benefit there can be to the imāmate of an Imām who has not yet reached the age of majority, to his subsequent occultation, and to the prolongation of his lifespan beyond its natural limits? And when they cannot attain to any answers which are convincing in their efficacy to and harmony with their *worldly* interests and considerations, they dismiss these realities in their entirety, even though there are numerous rational, historical and scriptural reasons and evidence which militate for this belief.

If we examine the conception of Mahdism as conceived by the *Ahl al-Bayt* with precision, we will find that the conception of this concept is much more comprehensive and more perfected than the concept which is offered by the followers of the School of the Caliphs in terms of this-worldly considerations. For example, the prolongation of the lifespan of Imām Mahdī enables him to be witness to and experience all the events that have occurred in the history of the world, so that he will be able to put his millennial experiences to use when he forms his universal order.

On the other hand, this extended period of occultation provides the opportunity for human society to progress in the hard sciences and in the humanities, and to experience a variety of forms of government, and eventually to reach the conclusion that in order for justice and equity to prevail, it is necessary for there to be an order whose constitution is premised on divine revelations and principles which is headed by one who is learned and experienced and who is divinely appointed. This idea is based on the belief that God uses specific means for the establishment of justice and equity on earth. As with everything else, God uses the logic of cause and effect for the establishment of justice and equity as He is averse to using other than normal means for putting things in motion. Of course this Divine convention does not preclude the occasional involvement on His part in the affairs of the world and His coming to the aid of the believers and His placing fear and dread in the hearts of the unbelievers (or, to give a couple of examples, to save Abraham ﷺ from the fire or to still the hand of the Jew who had held a sword over the head of the Most Noble Prophet ﷺ, so as to prevent him from being able to murder the Prophet ﷺ).

Thus, given this vantage, we see that the way in which social change progresses is a gradual process for which special conditions and circumstances are required; and such special circumstances are required in order for humanity to be saved from the dark night of tyranny and oppression that it has been possessed with; and another special circumstances is required for it to be guided toward equity and justice and divine guidance and light. That is the advent of a unique leader who is to appear when it is deemed by God ﷻ that the circumstances for his advent are right. The right material conditions must obtain so that the call to justice of Imām Mahdī ﷺ can reach everyone's ears immediately.

It is also possible for us to look at the benefits of the belief in Mahdism as conceived by the *Ahl al-Bayt* ﷺ from a different angle. Our position is that the belief in a conception of messianism which entails a savior who is veiled from view but who is alive and who has an influence on the currents in society which affect the believers and who is endowed with all the attributes and characteristics of the imāmate such as immaculacy and being the perfected embodiment of knowledge and action, will foster a special state of emotional and spiritual alacrity in society. To understand that there exists a link which connects the world to the heavens gives one a good sense of confidence and assurance, and once one understands this unique conception of Mahdism and attains to faith and certainty in it by way of his reason, a unique feeling of peace and contentment comes over him.

The belief in a Mahdism which maintains that the Twelfth Imām has been appointed by God by way of His Prophet with the specific attributes necessary for taking on the burden of responsibility of the imāmate and is present and is watching over the acts of humanity and all of the social and political currents that take place around the globe fosters the belief in the hearts of men that above all of the various governments and social and political currents, there is a higher integral divine order, and that God's representative on earth monitors all of these activities. This belief is spiritually uplifting and gives hope to those who are oppressed and are awaiting their savior.

This relationship is strengthened when, during the Lesser Occultation, people were in touch with their Imām by way of the Four Deputies; and is similarly strengthened during the Greater Occultation when people are in touch with and maintain their relationships with the fully-qualified magisters (*foqahā*) of sound moral character, and specifically with the fully-empowered *Valī-e Faqīh*, who is the general representative of the Lord of the Age

Islamic Messianism

ﷻ. Given these conditions, one feels that the imāmate has manifested itself in the form of the *Valī-e Faqīh* and seeks to revivify and implement the sacred ordinances of Islam. Therefore, the Mahdism which is offered by the *Ahl al-Bayt* ﷺ is a dynamic, effective and positive Mahdism which is capable of confronting the social and political realities of human existence, whereas the Mahdism that is maintained by those who were ideologically loyal to the dynastic caliphs in preference to the Purified Members of the Household of the Prophet ﷺ has no effect on these critical realities of human existence and is nothing more than a prophecy about the future.

The nature of the Mahdism which is presented by the *Ahl al-Bayt* ﷺ is such that it encourages and inspires people to be active in the cause of bringing about the preconditions necessary for the advent of the Mahdī ﷻ, and gives them the sense of assurance that they have a Master who is aware of them and who watches over them; and given this, the Expectation of the Advent does not take on the overtones and connotations of muteness, defeat and helplessness in the face of tyranny and oppression and injustice, but rather, means activity, commotion and striving for the establishment of the conditions necessary for the advent of the Awaited Imām al-Mahdī ﷻ.

Summary
We can sum up the discussion in the following points:

1. Religion is a more comprehensive interpretation and expression of the reality of the human condition; and Islam is the more comprehensive interpretation and expression of the verities of religion; and Shī'a Islam is the more comprehensive interpretation and expression of the truth of Islam. Consequently, the messianism or Mahdism which the *Ahl al-Bayt* have introduced and promoted is the most perfected form of the messianic principle in which all Muslims are united in their belief.

2. The principle and basic difference between the *Ahl al-Bayt*'s conception of messianism (or the coming of the universal messiah) and the conceptions of other denominations and sects lies in the question of the imāmate. In the School of the *Ahl al-Bayt*, this savior is a real person who is the Twelfth Imām and Successor to the Prophet, whereas the Mahdī as conceived by the followers of the caliphs is simply and purely a prophecy concerning some abstract event in the future.

3. And *because* the coming of the universal savior is, from the point of view of the *Ahl al-Bayt*, concomitant with the advent of the Twelfth Imām who will have no successor, the Imām al-Mahdī must necessarily have the following three attributes:

a. His birth necessarily took place under conditions of strict secrecy.
   b. He was vested in the office of the imāmate while he was still a child.
   c. His occultation necessitates that he be given a long lifespan.

4. The above three attributes of the Imām al-Mahdī ﷻ have been proven and established beyond doubt by way of scriptural, rational and empirical (historical) proofs, and there are no logical or religious reasons that could act as obstacles to believing in them.

The messianic conception of Mahdism as conceived and introduced by the *Ahl al-Bayt* ﷺ and as promulgated by the School of the *Ahl al-Bayt* ﷺ is a more perfected form and expression of messianism (belief in the coming of the universal savior). It is a precious and perfecting belief of Divine origin which has numerous emotional, intellectual and spiritual benefits for humanity, gives us hope and inspires us to act in the cause of justice and uproots the hopelessness and despair engendered by tyranny and oppression. As such, the Shīʿa conception of Mahdism is fully in accord and in harmony with the social teachings of Islam.

www.ingramcontent.com/pod-product-compliance
Lightning Source LLC
Chambersburg PA
CBHW020320010526
44107CB00054B/1913